ALL RIGHTS RESERVED©
2024

No part of this publication may be reproduced, distributed, or transmitted in any form or by any means, including photocopying, recording, or other electronic or mechanical methods, without the prior written permission of the publisher, except for brief quotations incorporated in critical reviews and other specific noncommercial uses. Any unauthorized replica of this work is prohibited.

CHARLITTON LEOPOLDINO

Color test page

Use this page to test what the tone of your pencils, pens or brushes will look like

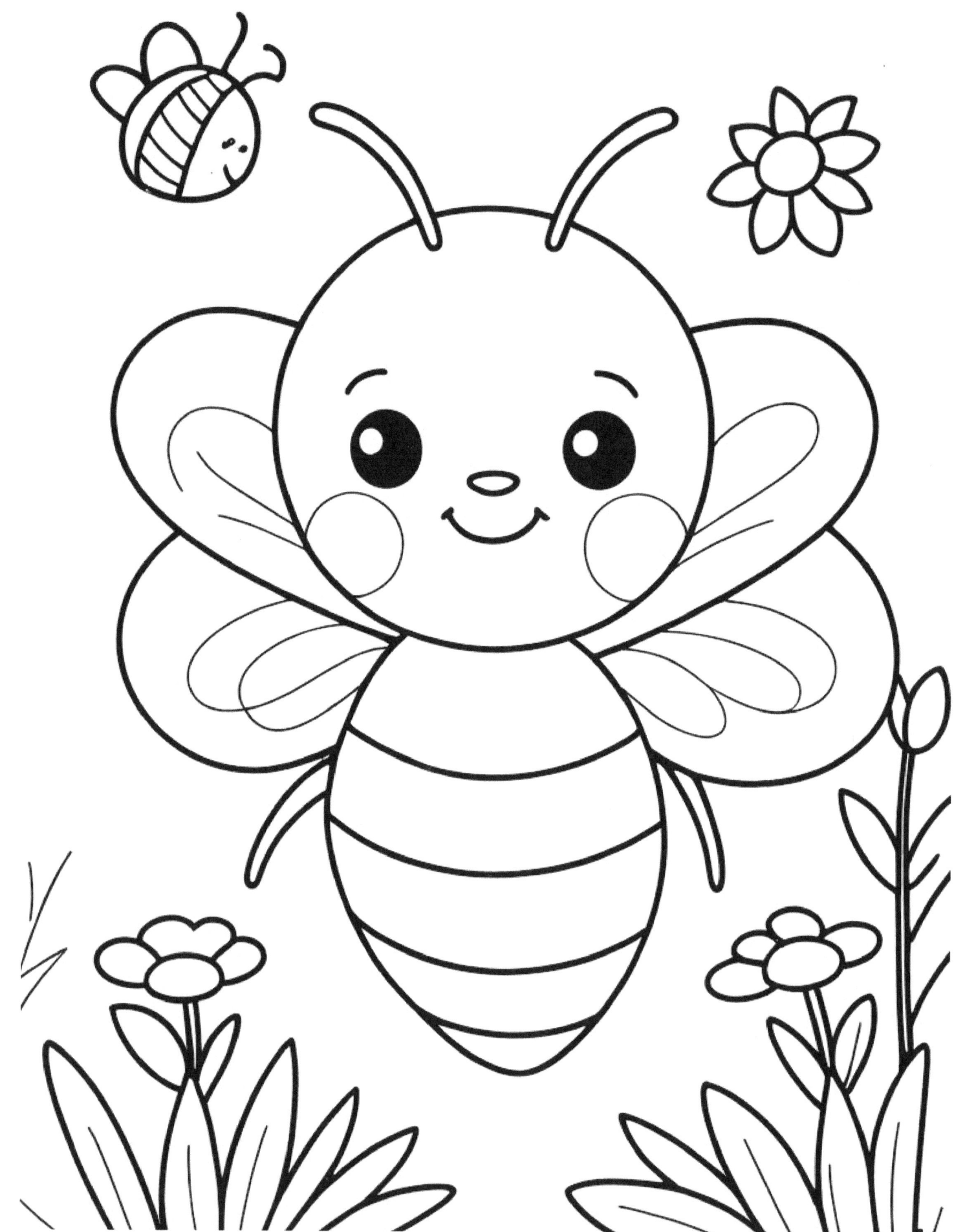

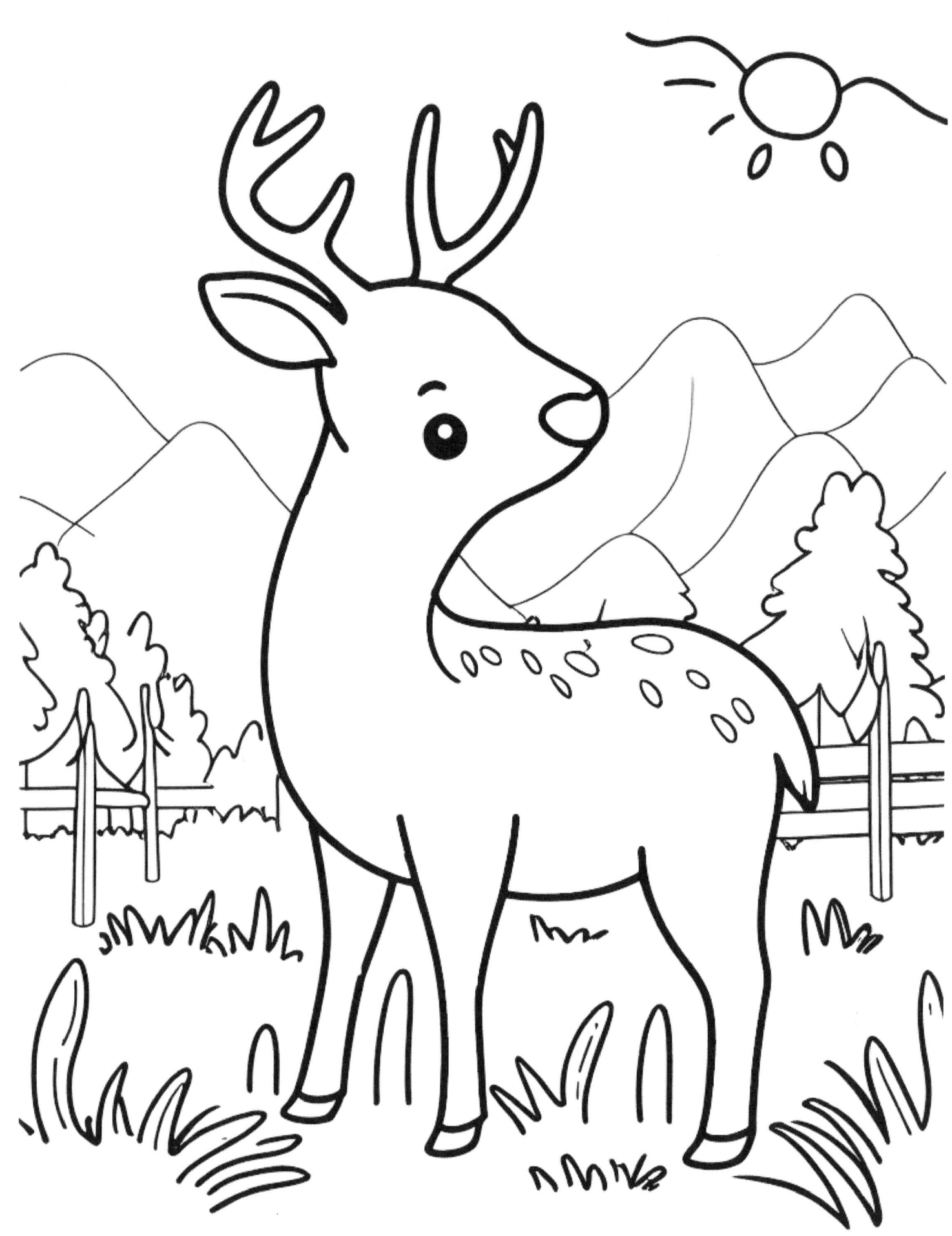

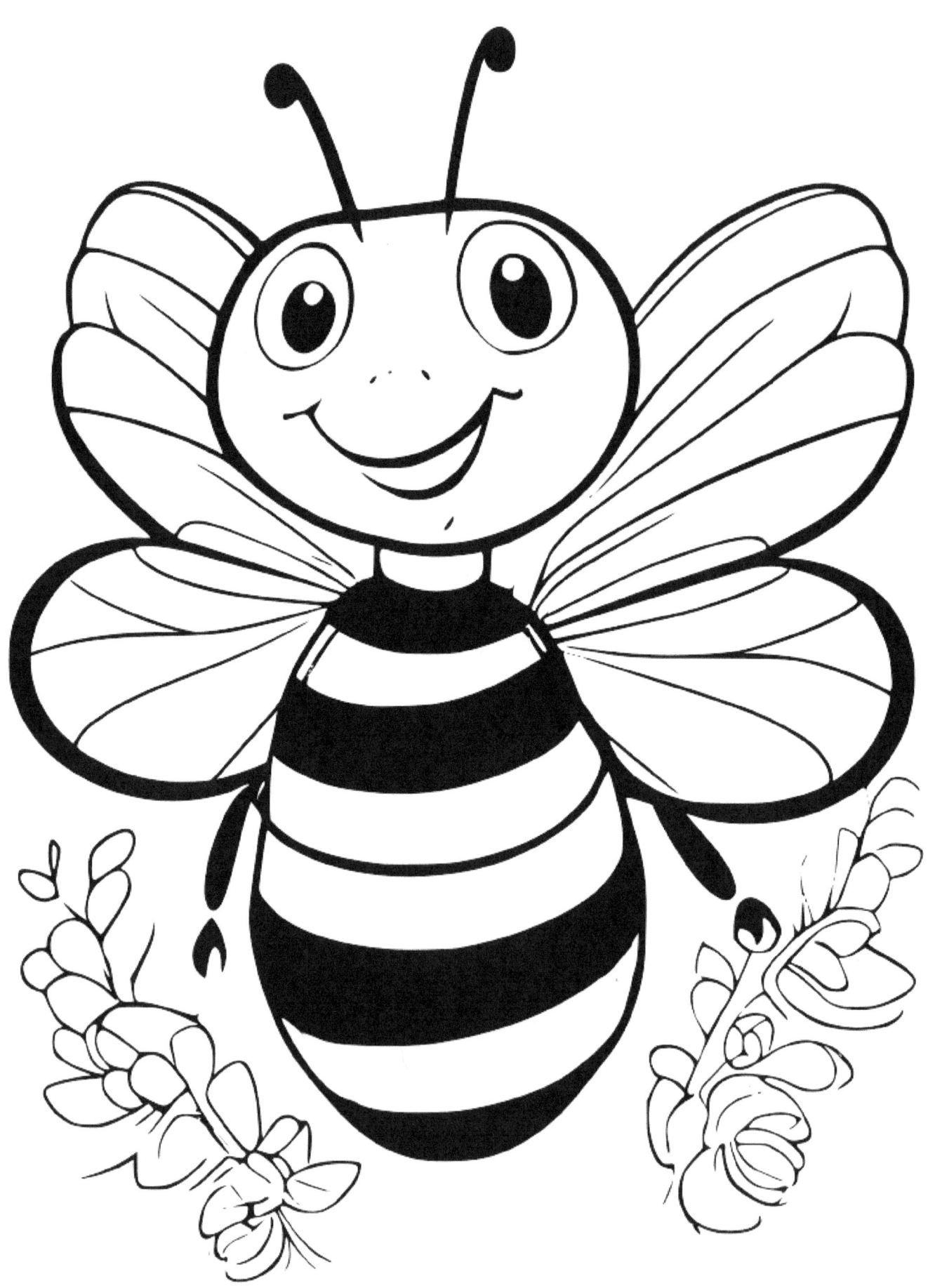

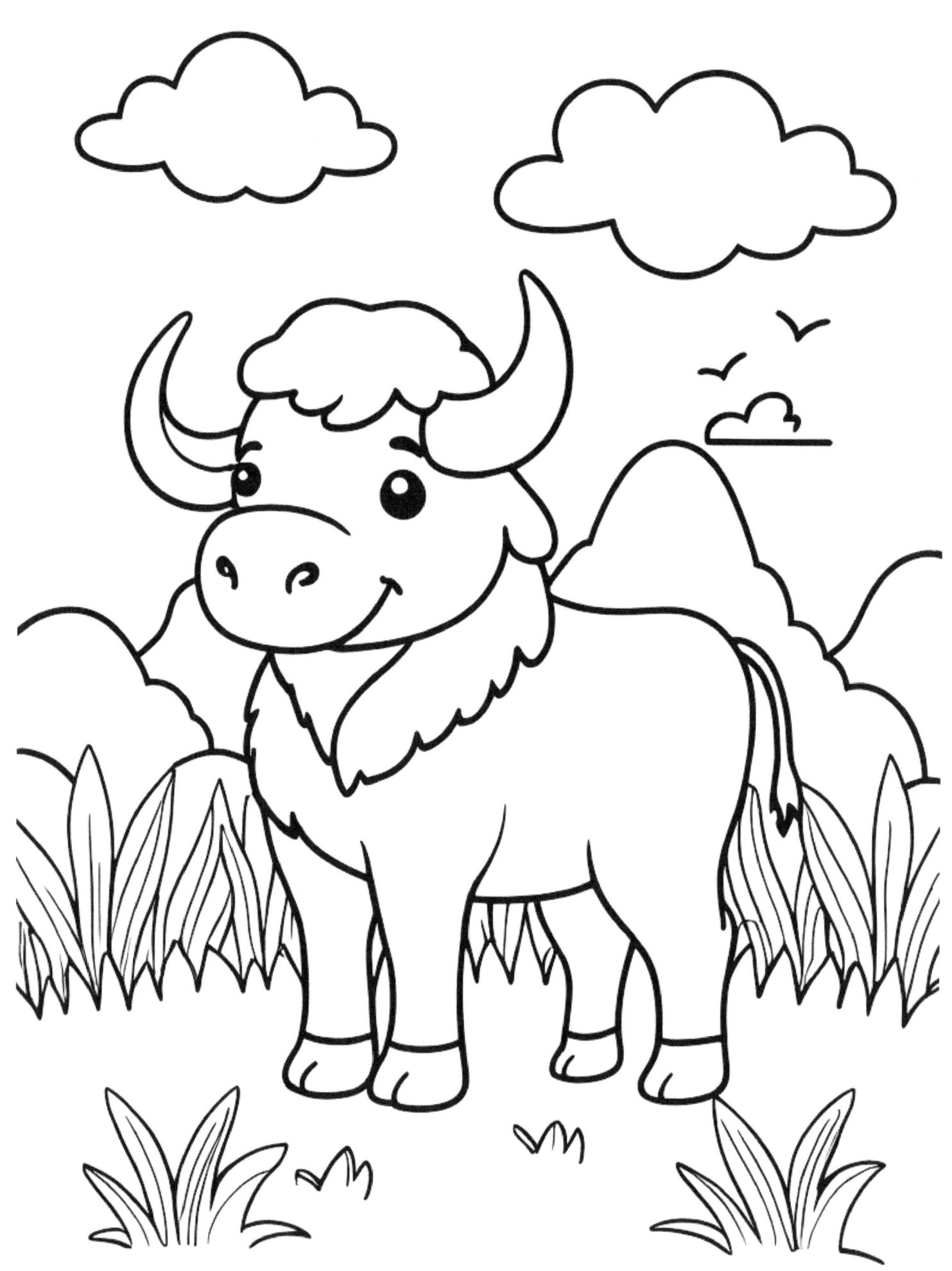

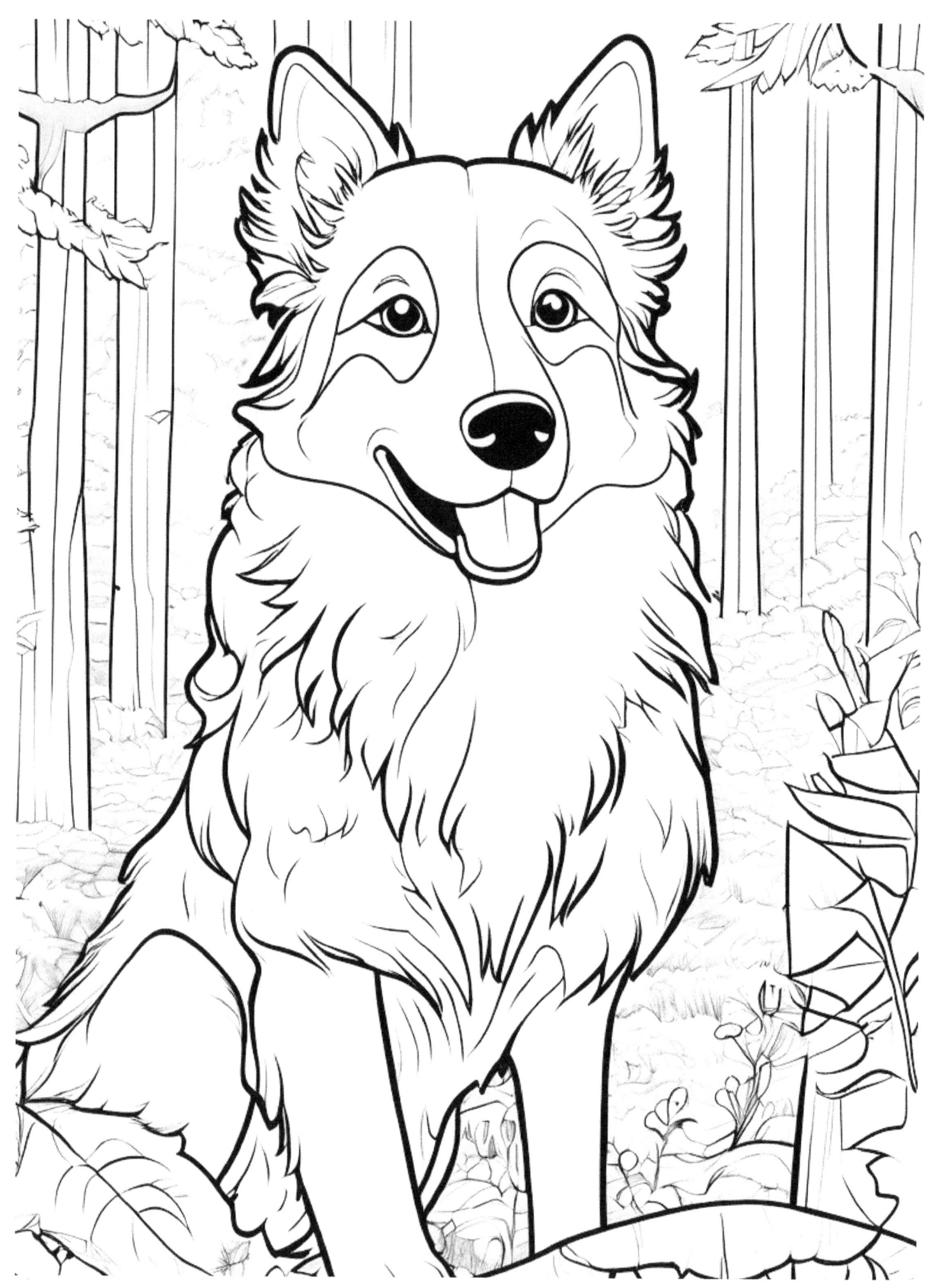

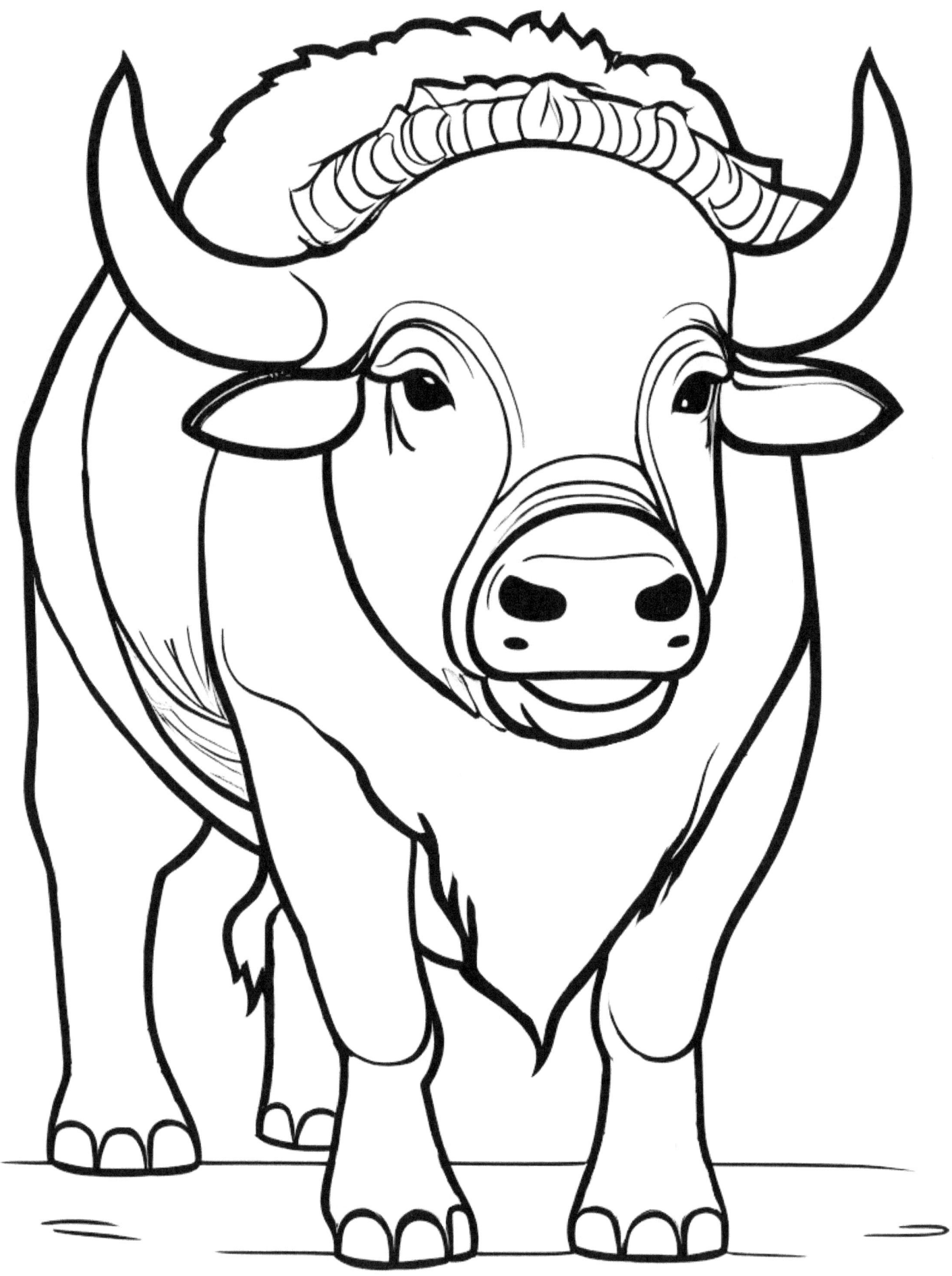

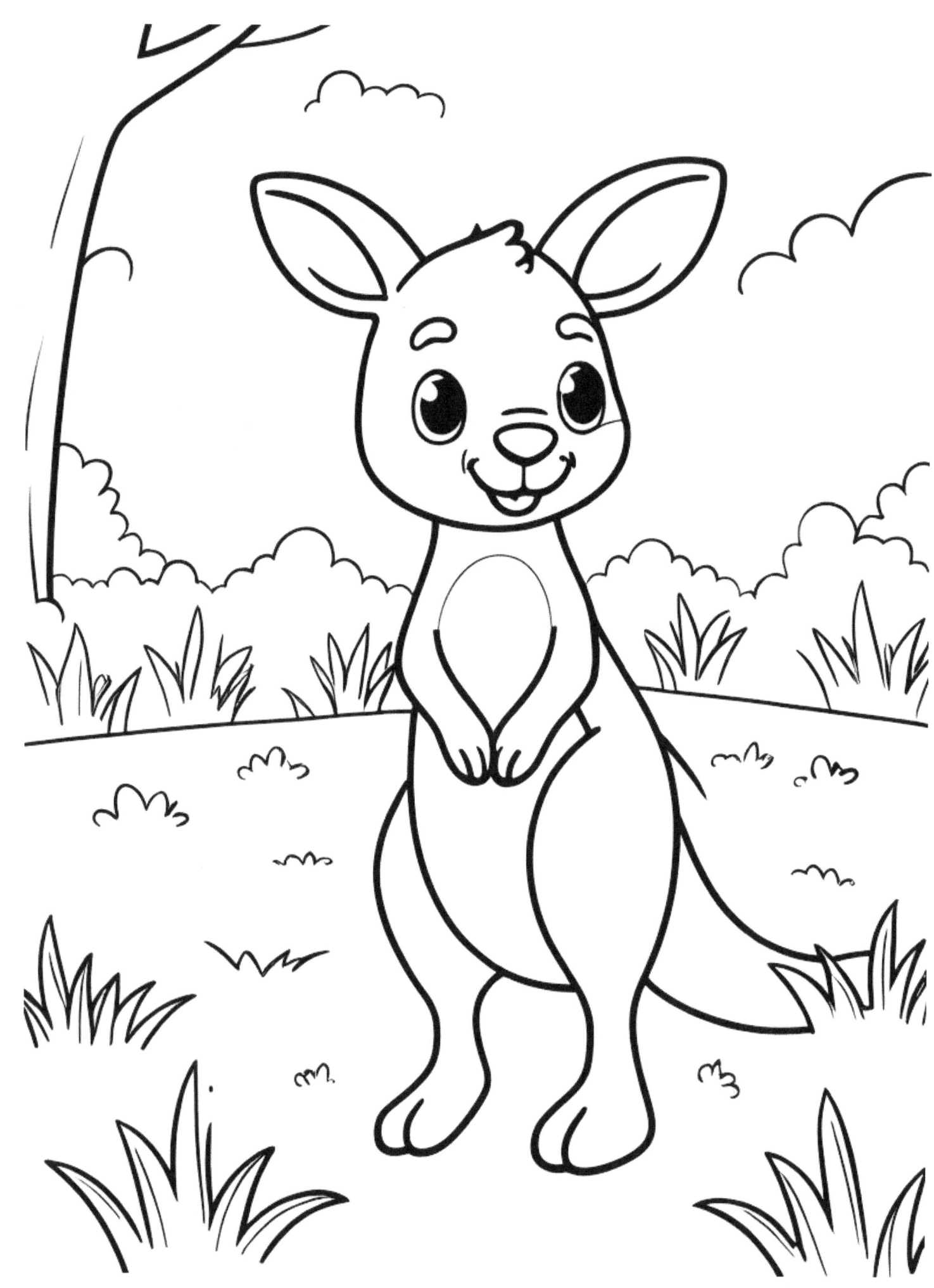

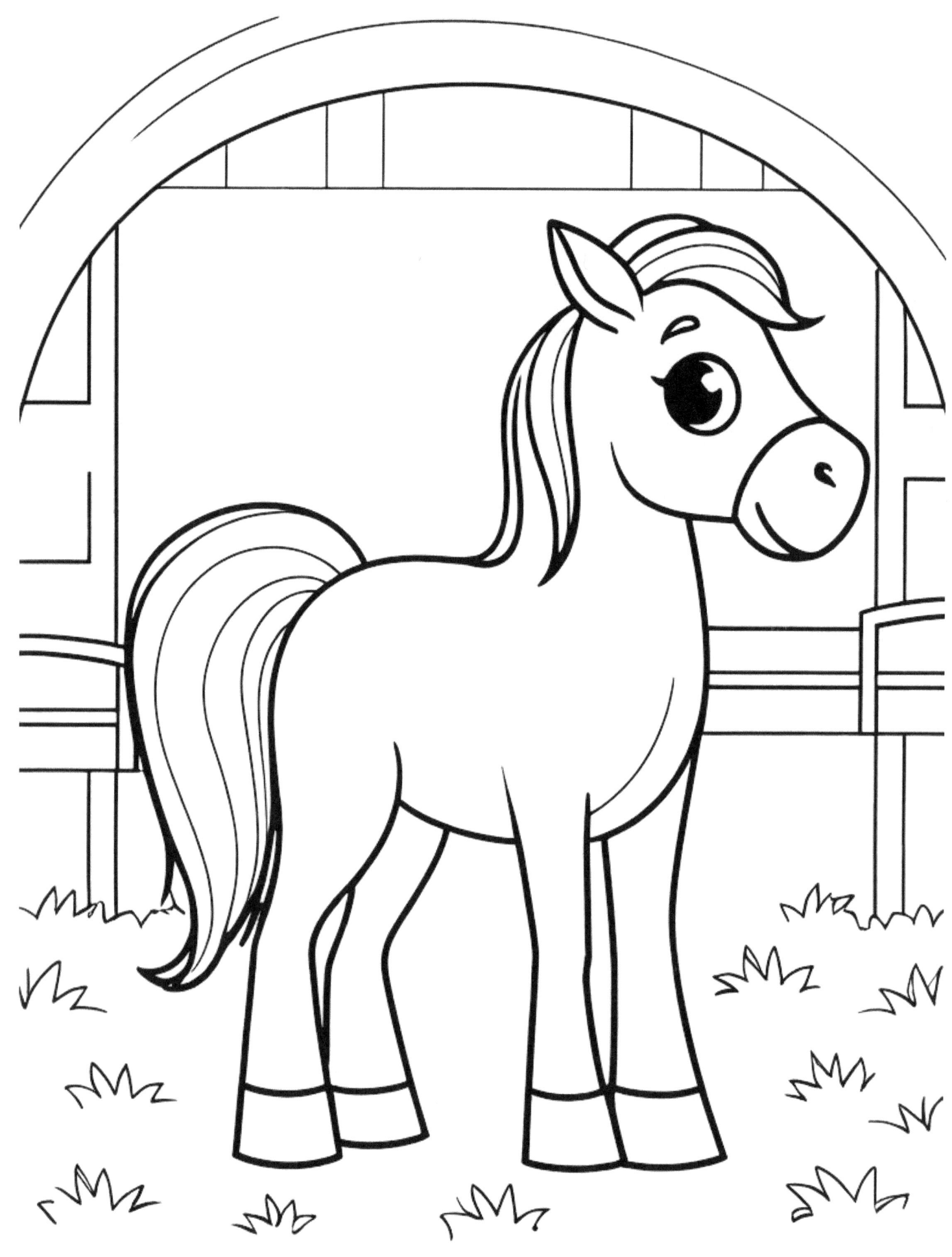

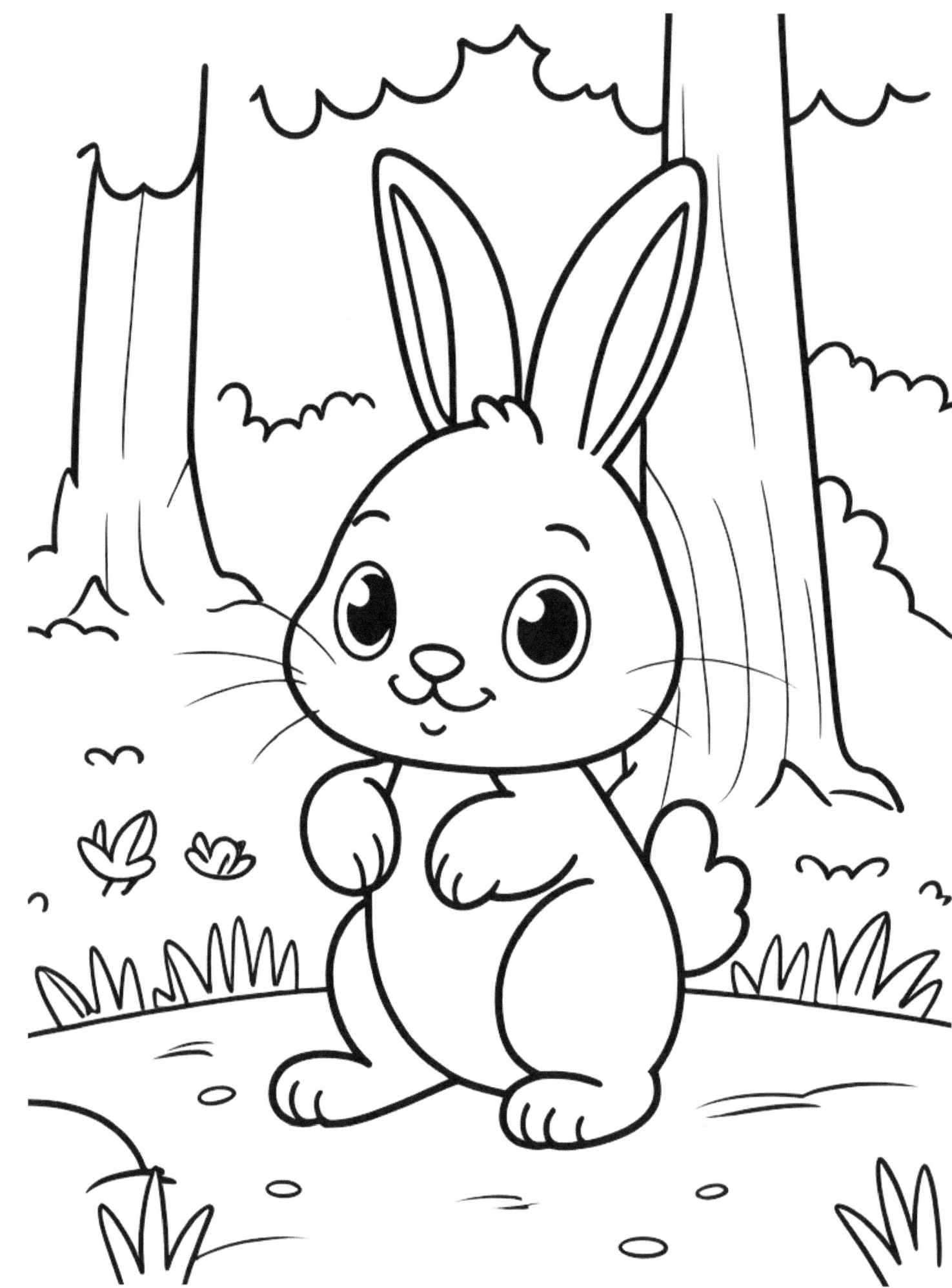

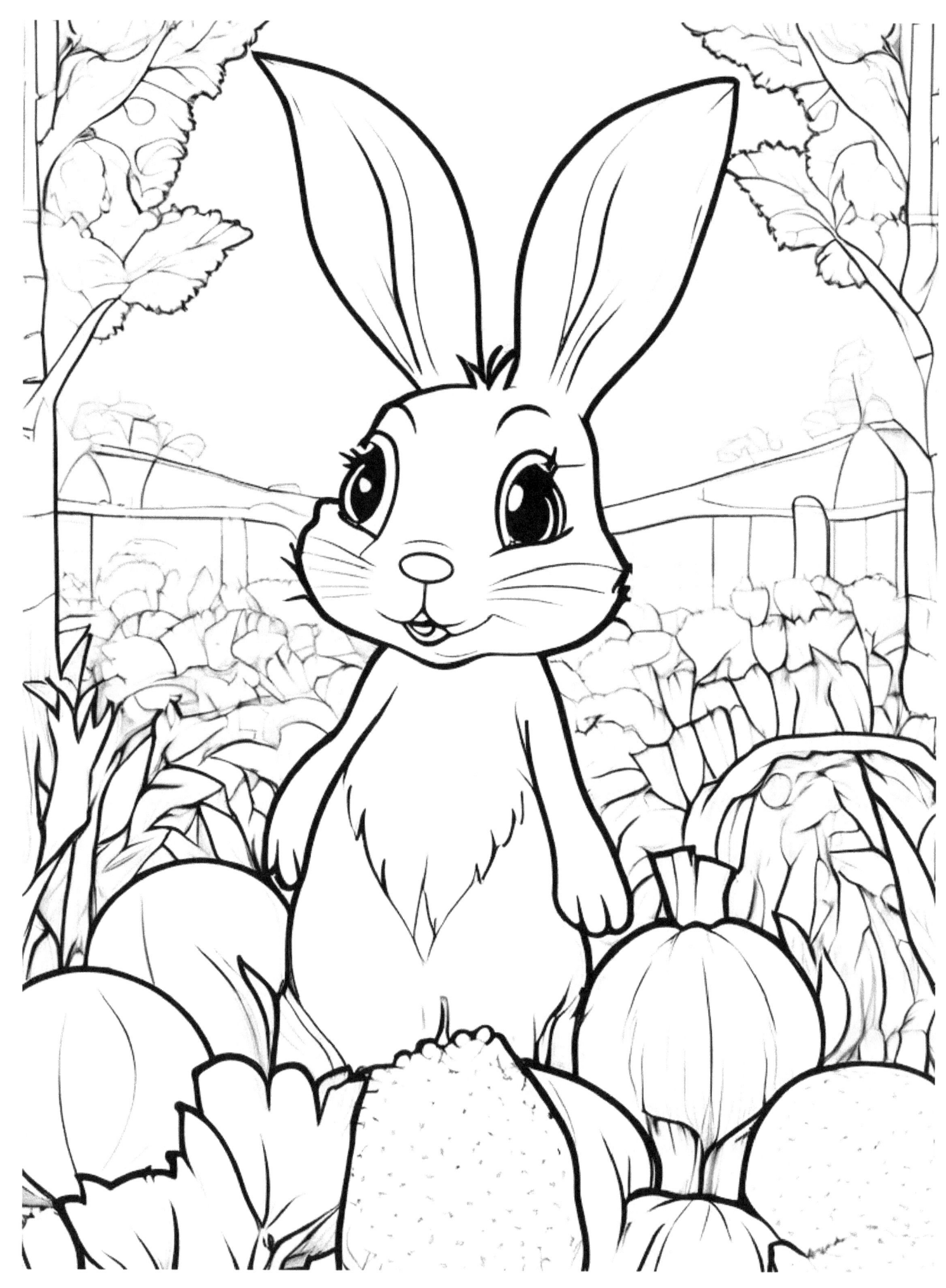

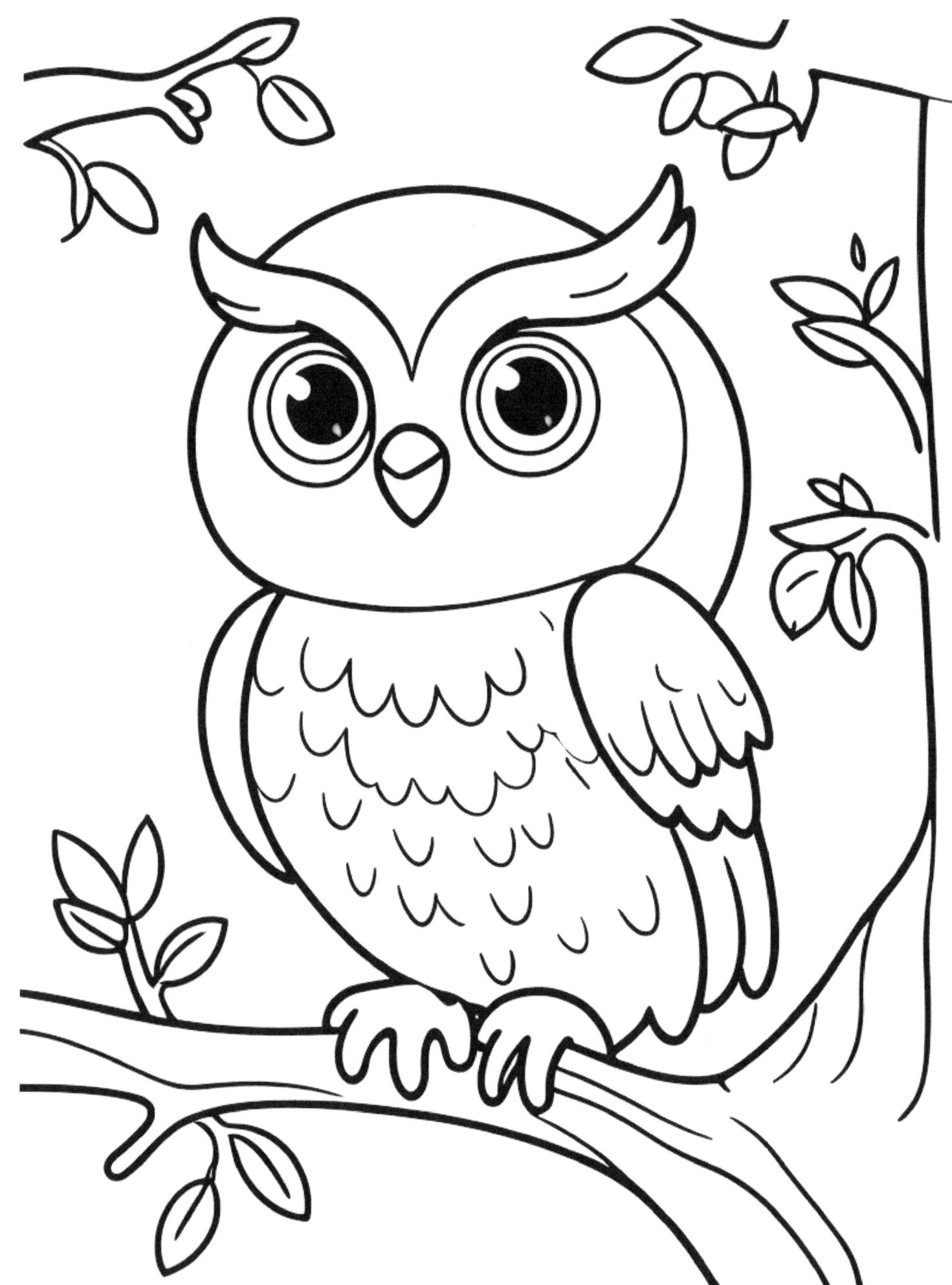

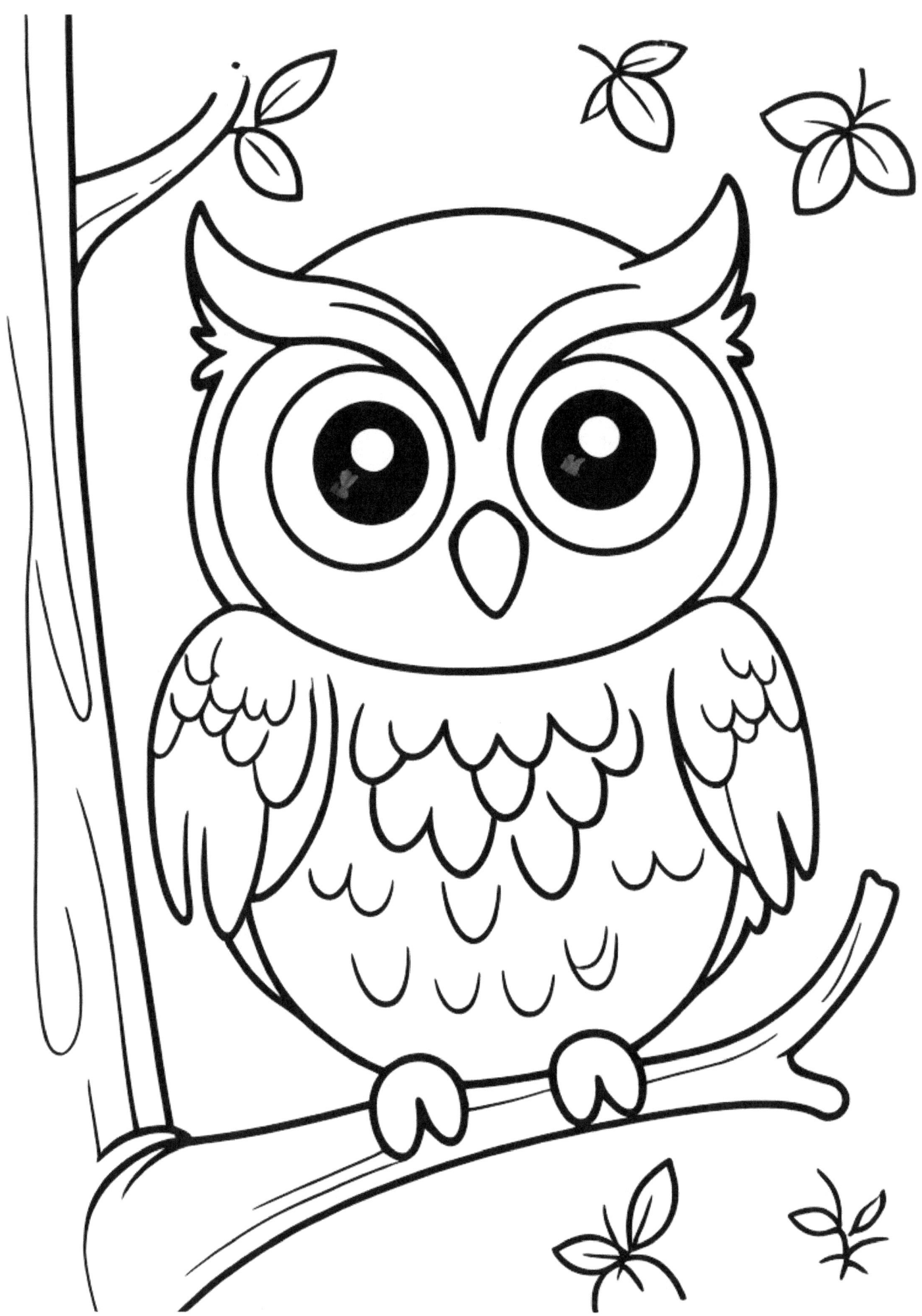

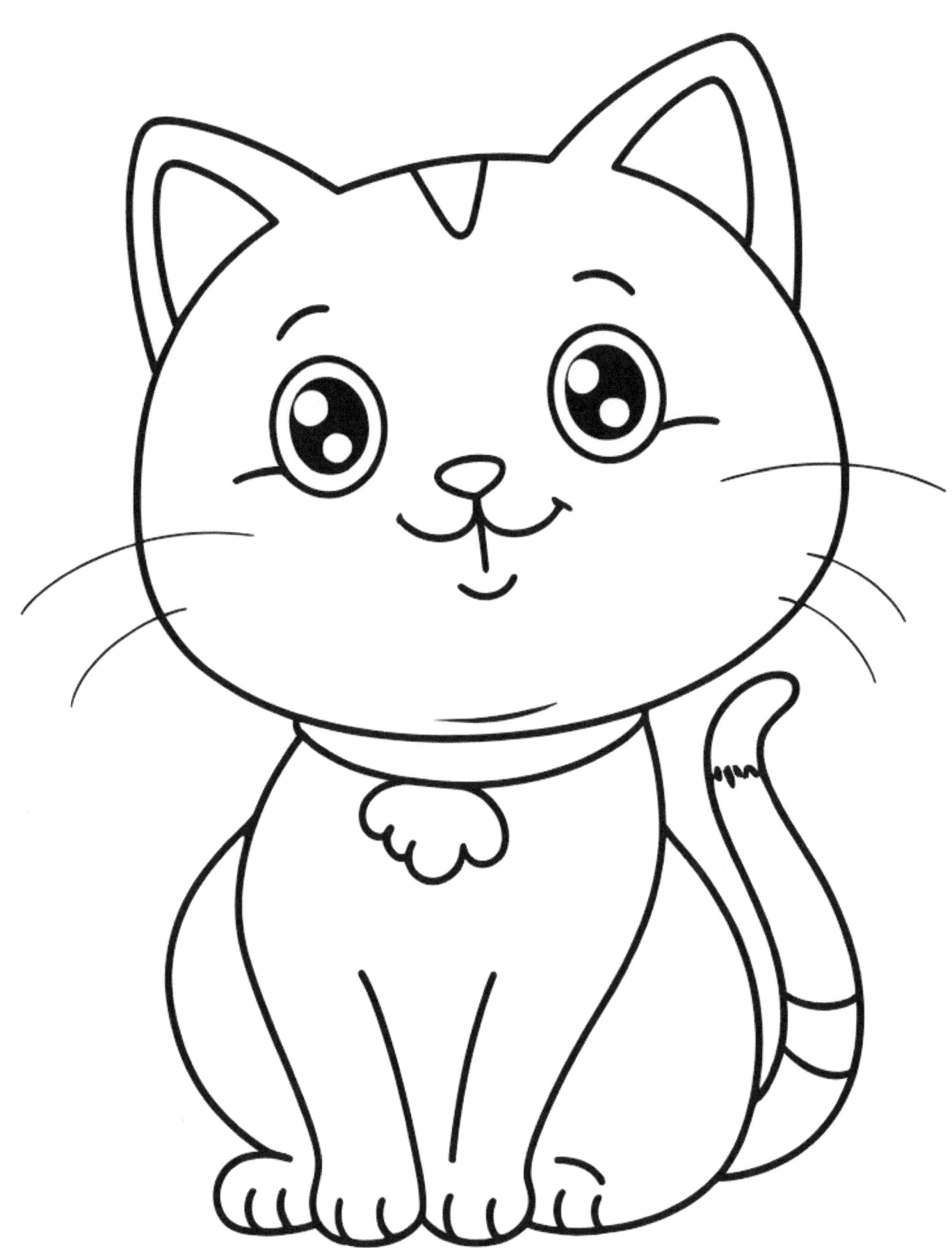

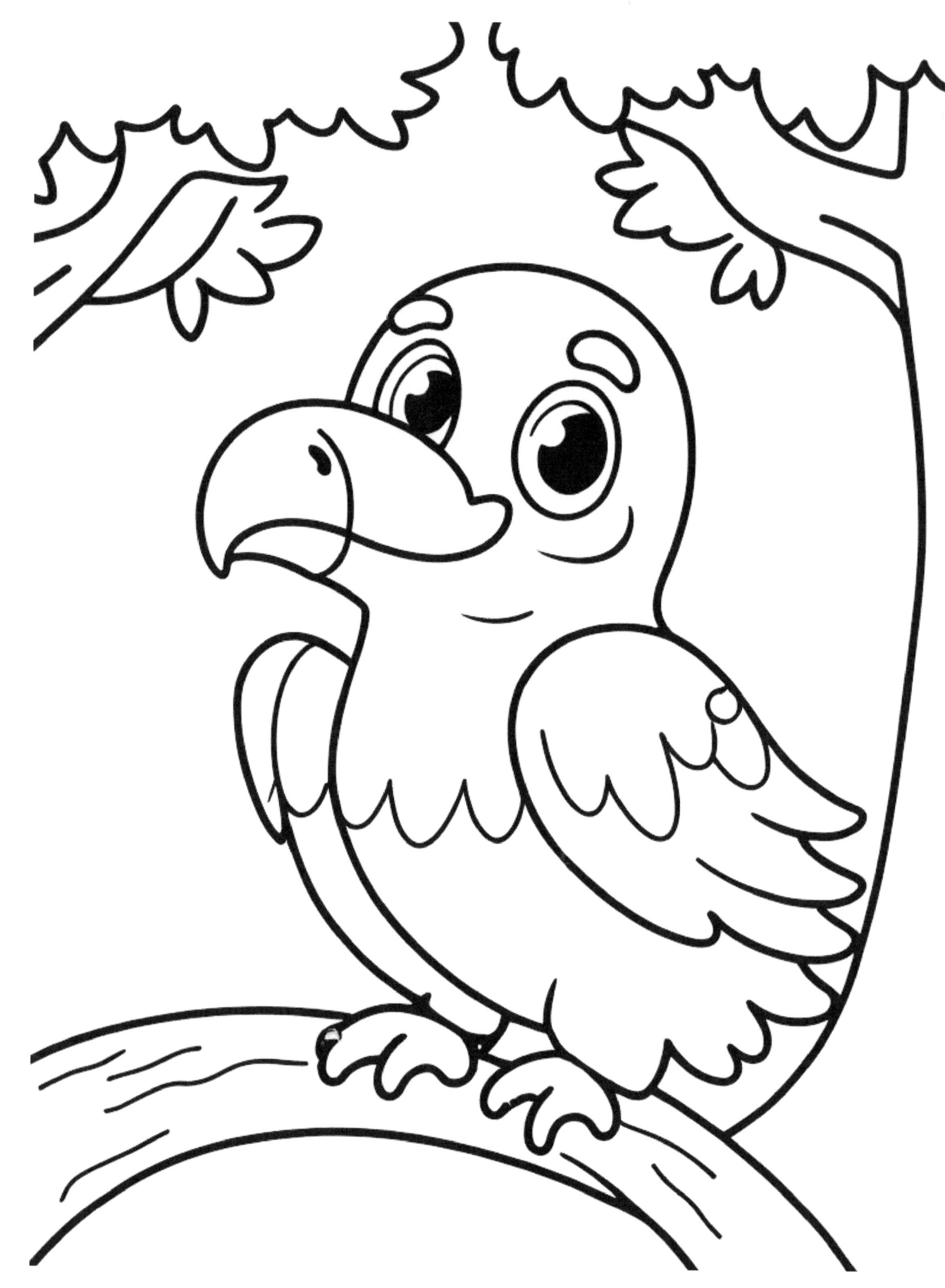

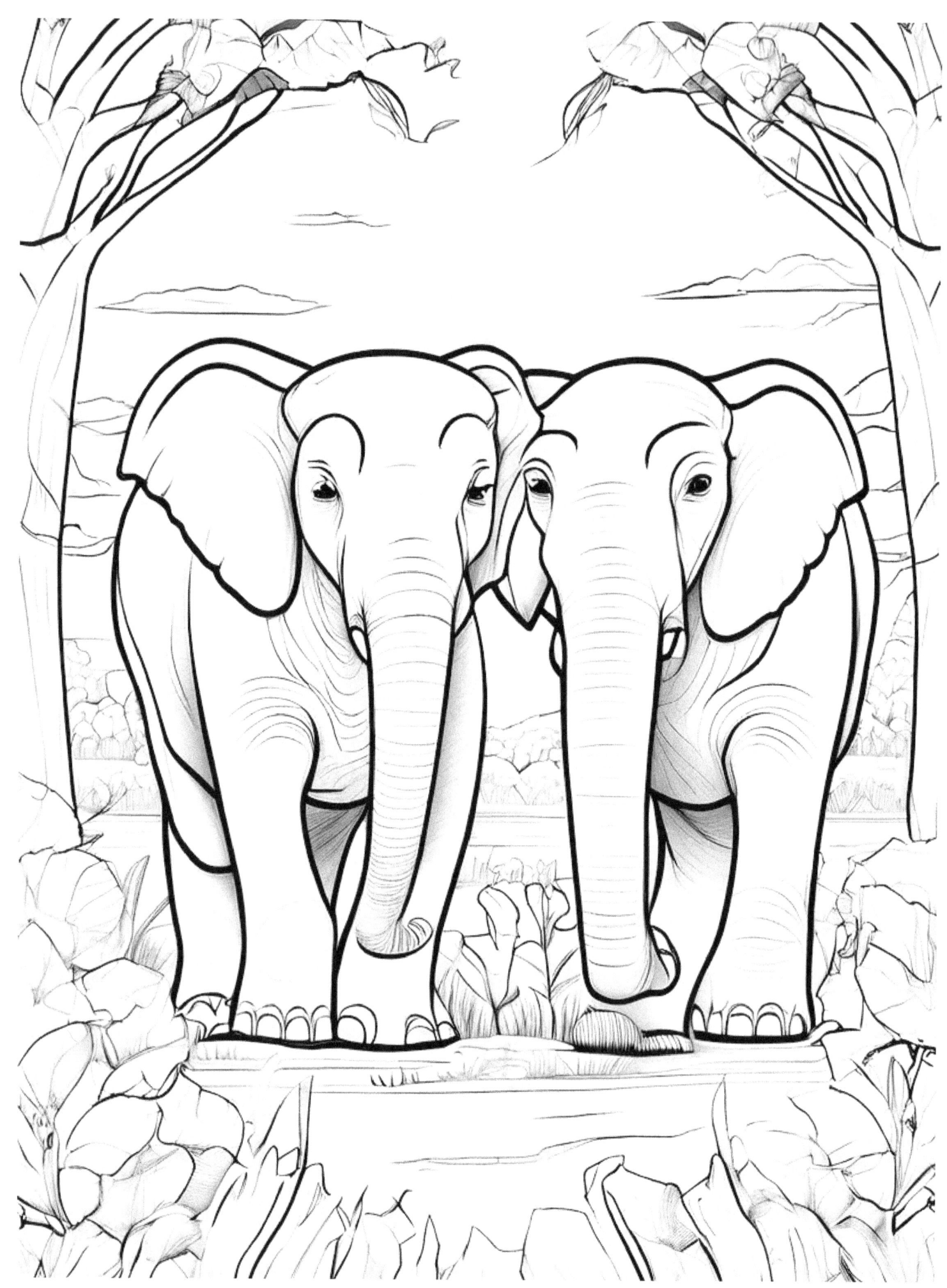

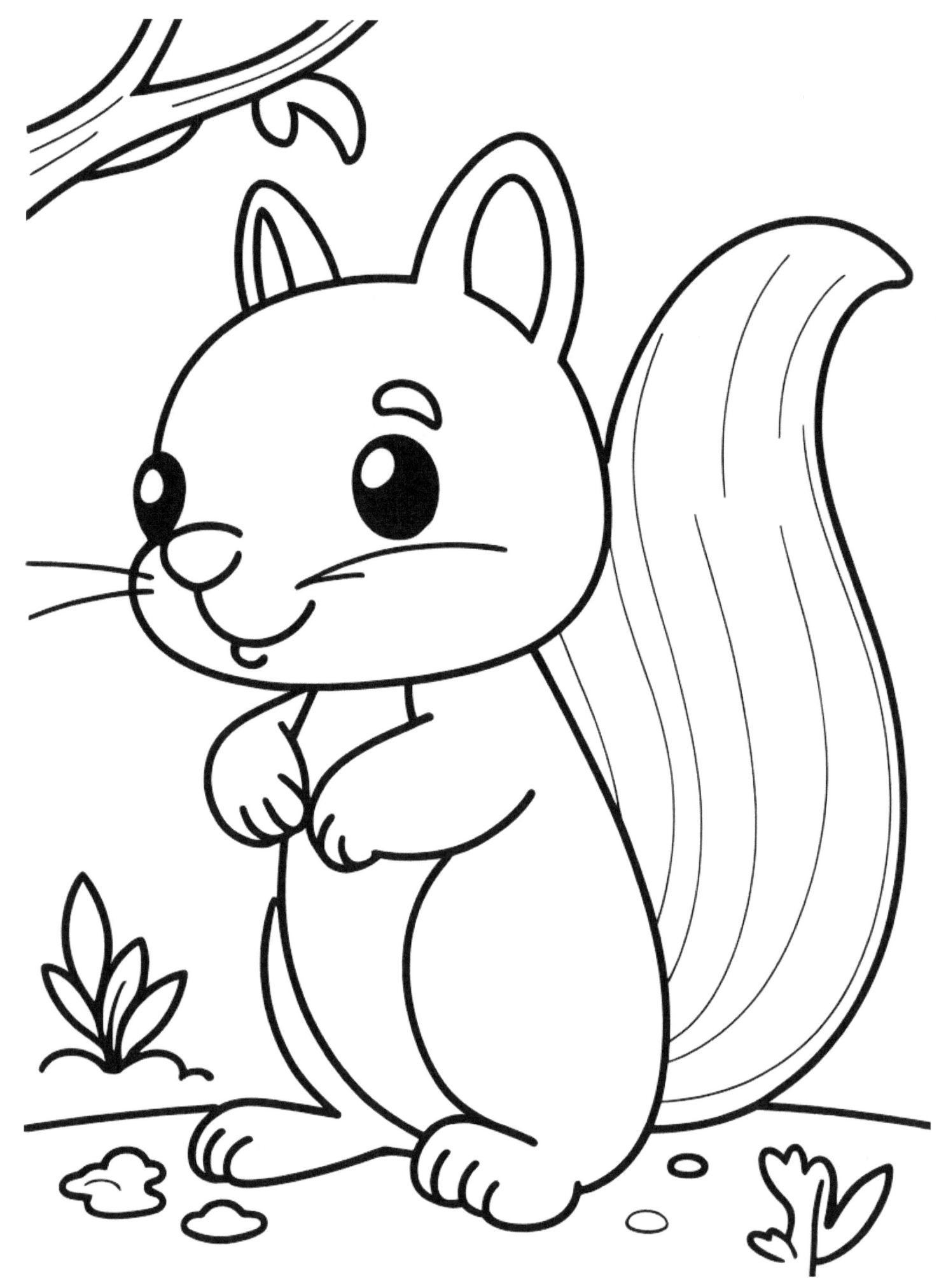

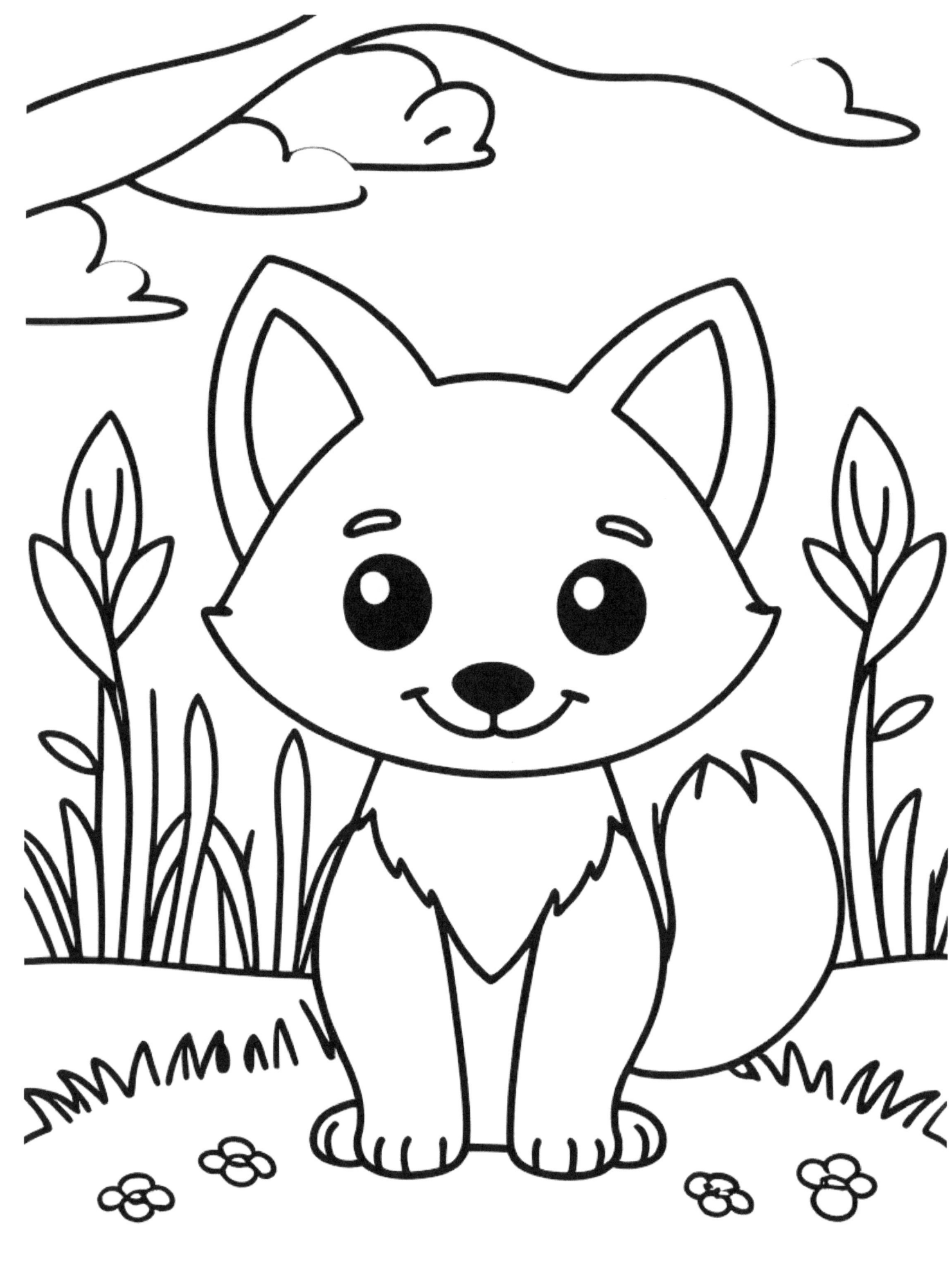

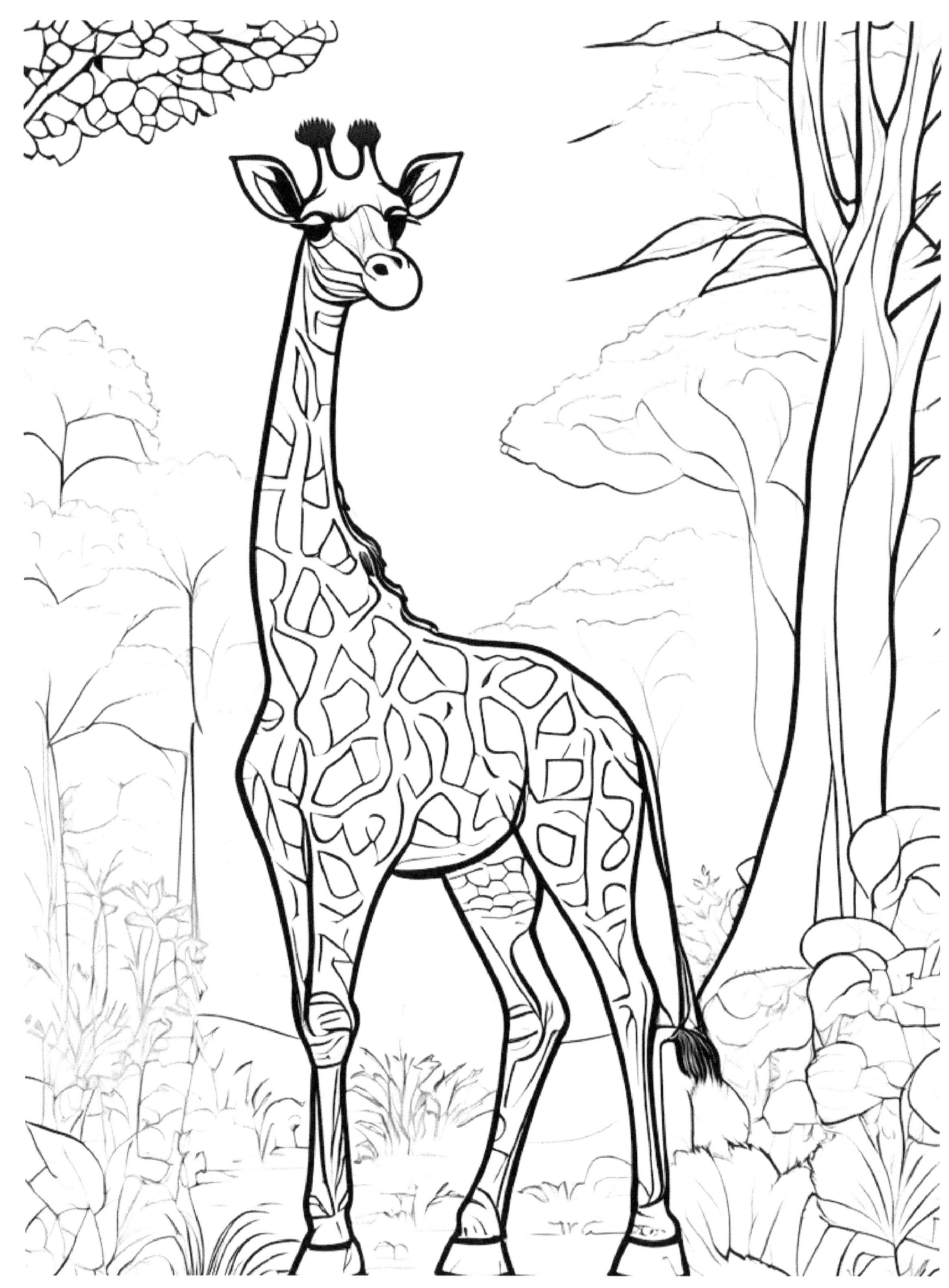

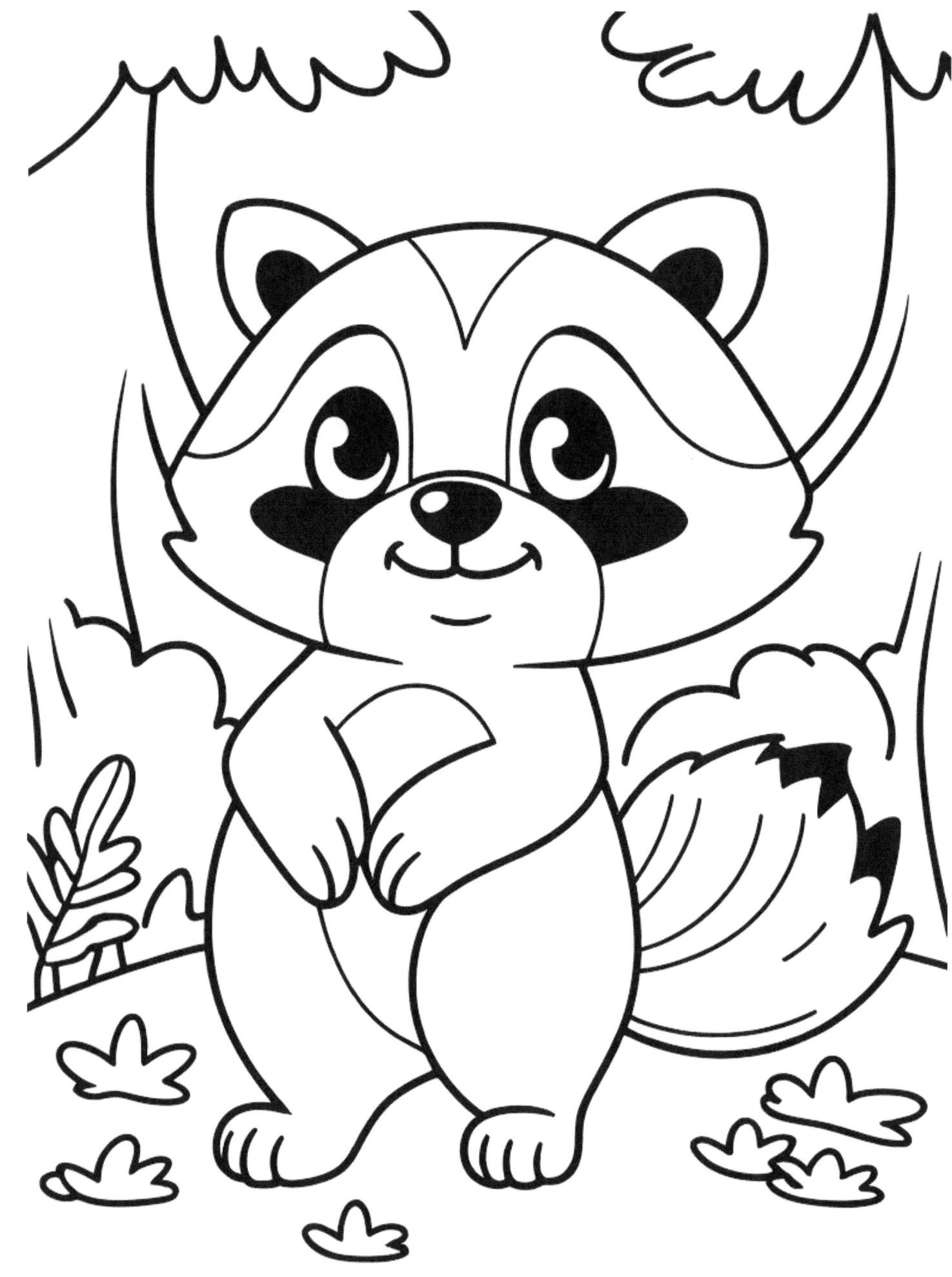

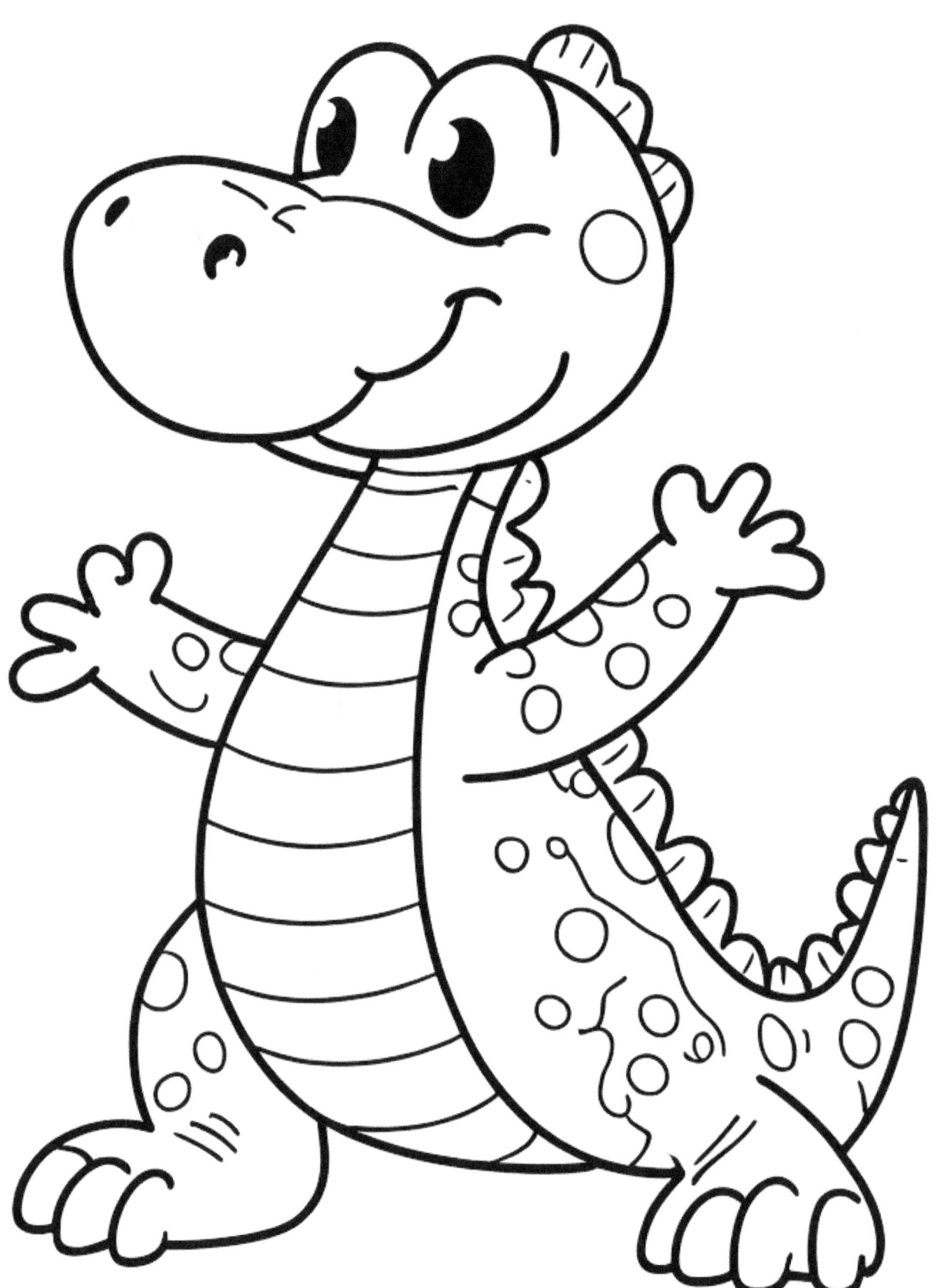

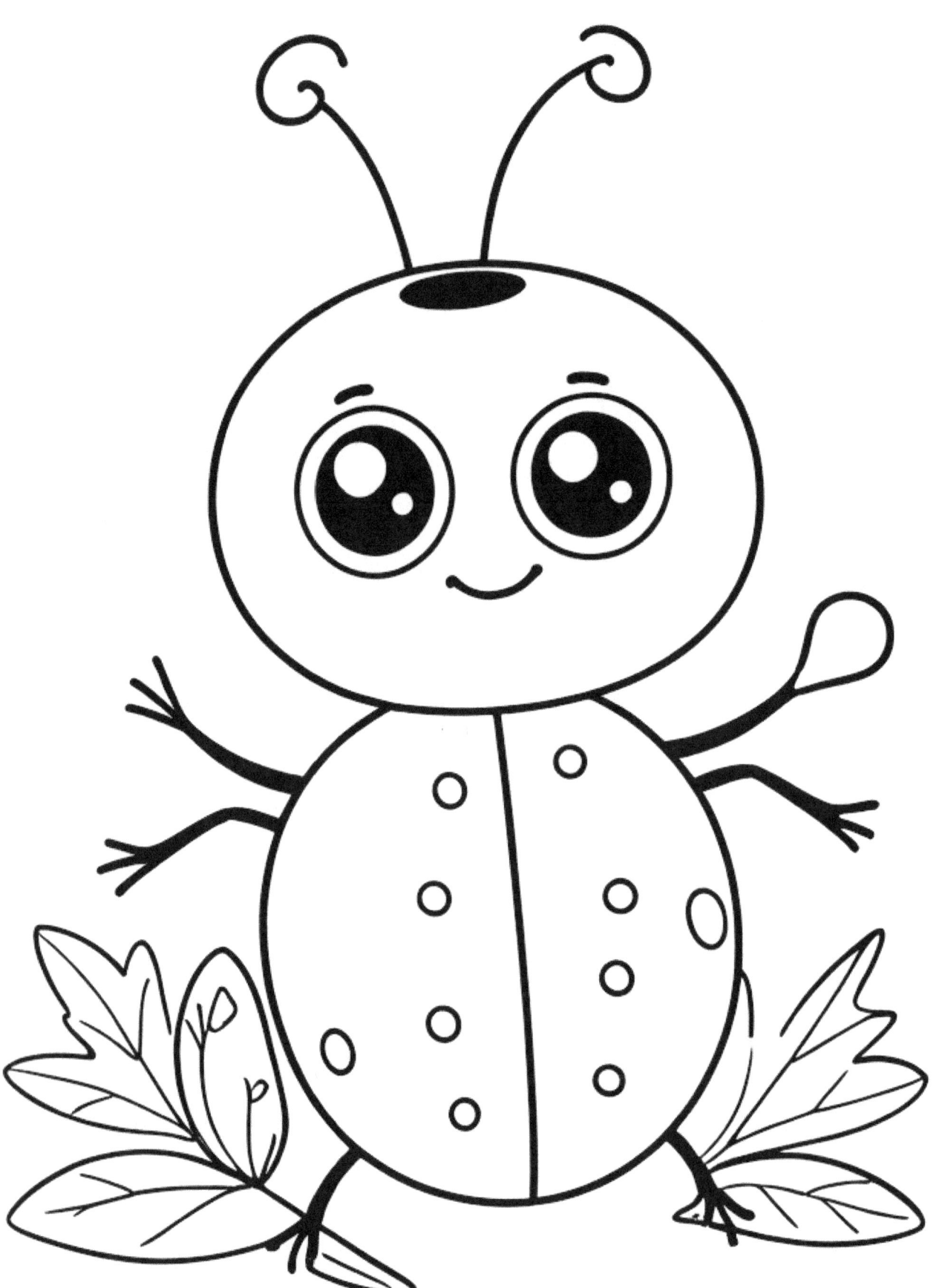

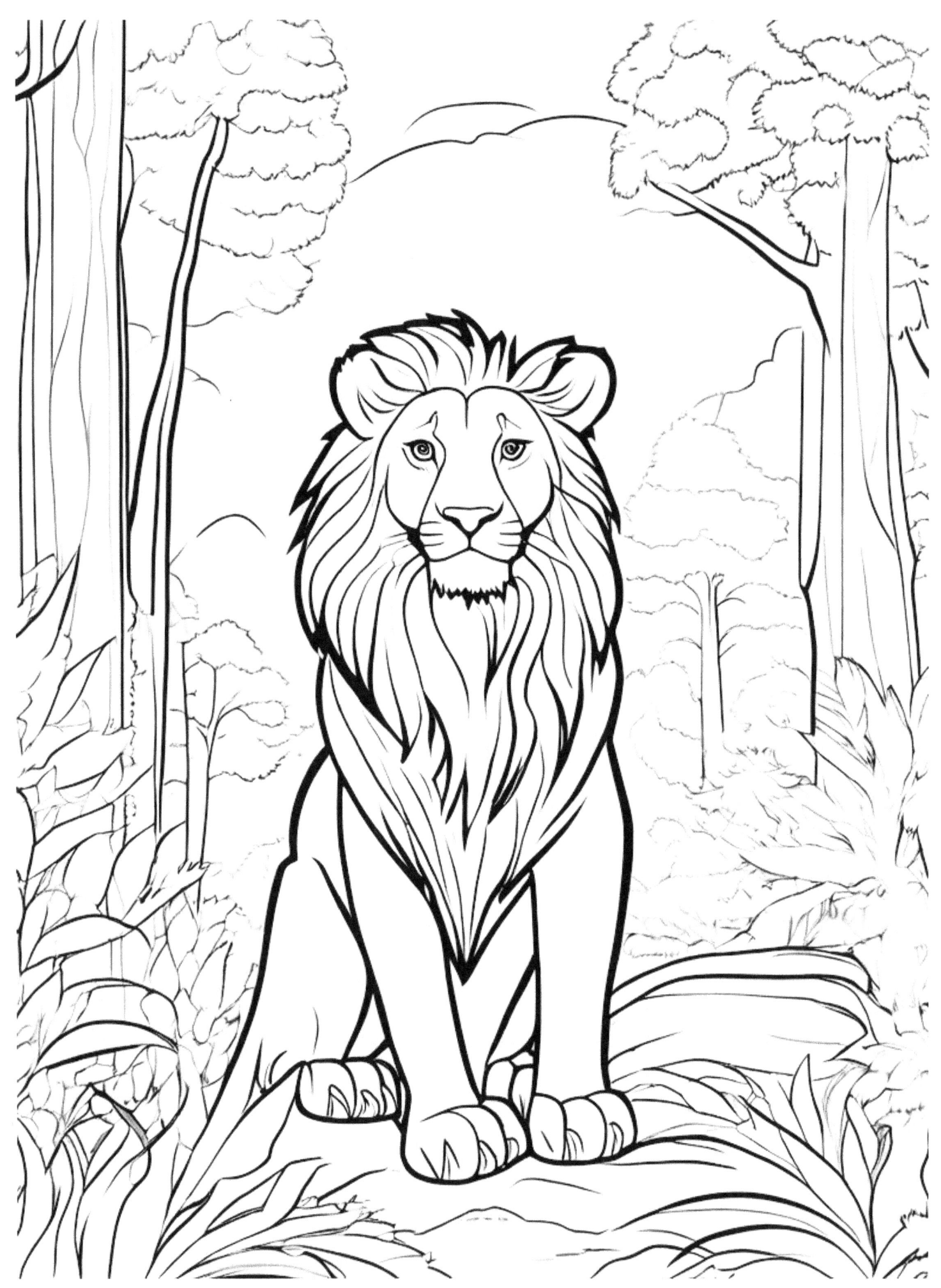

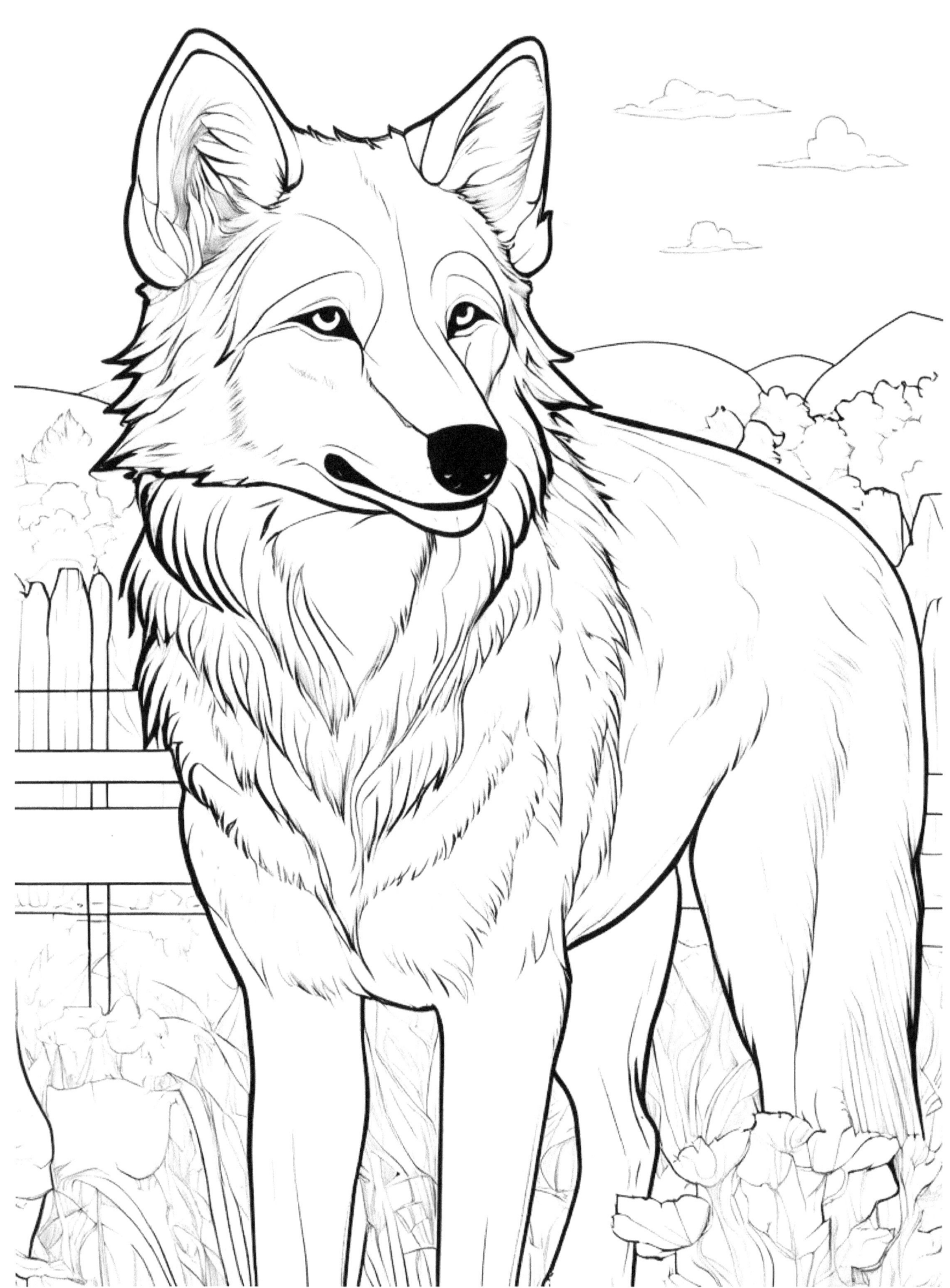

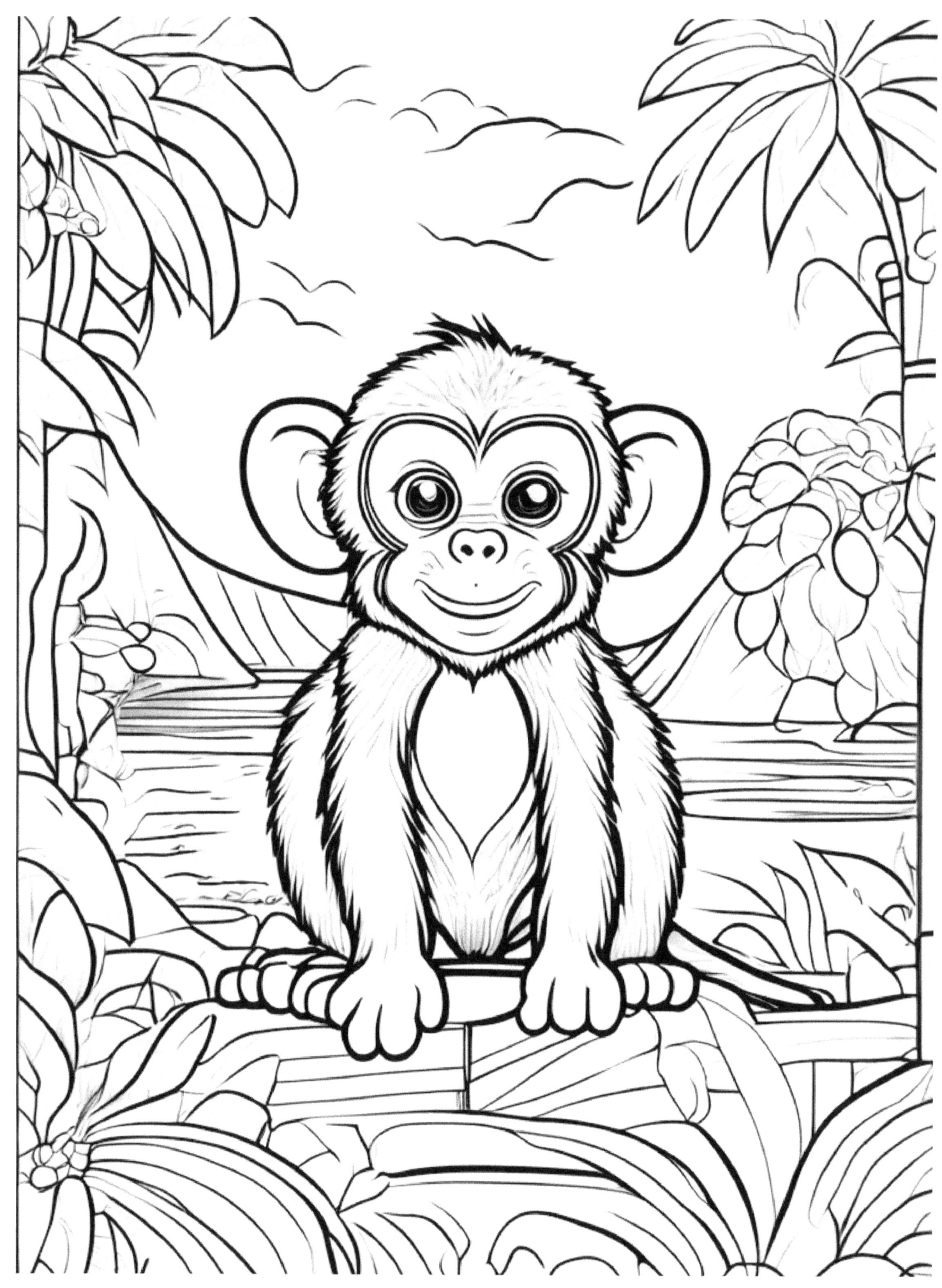

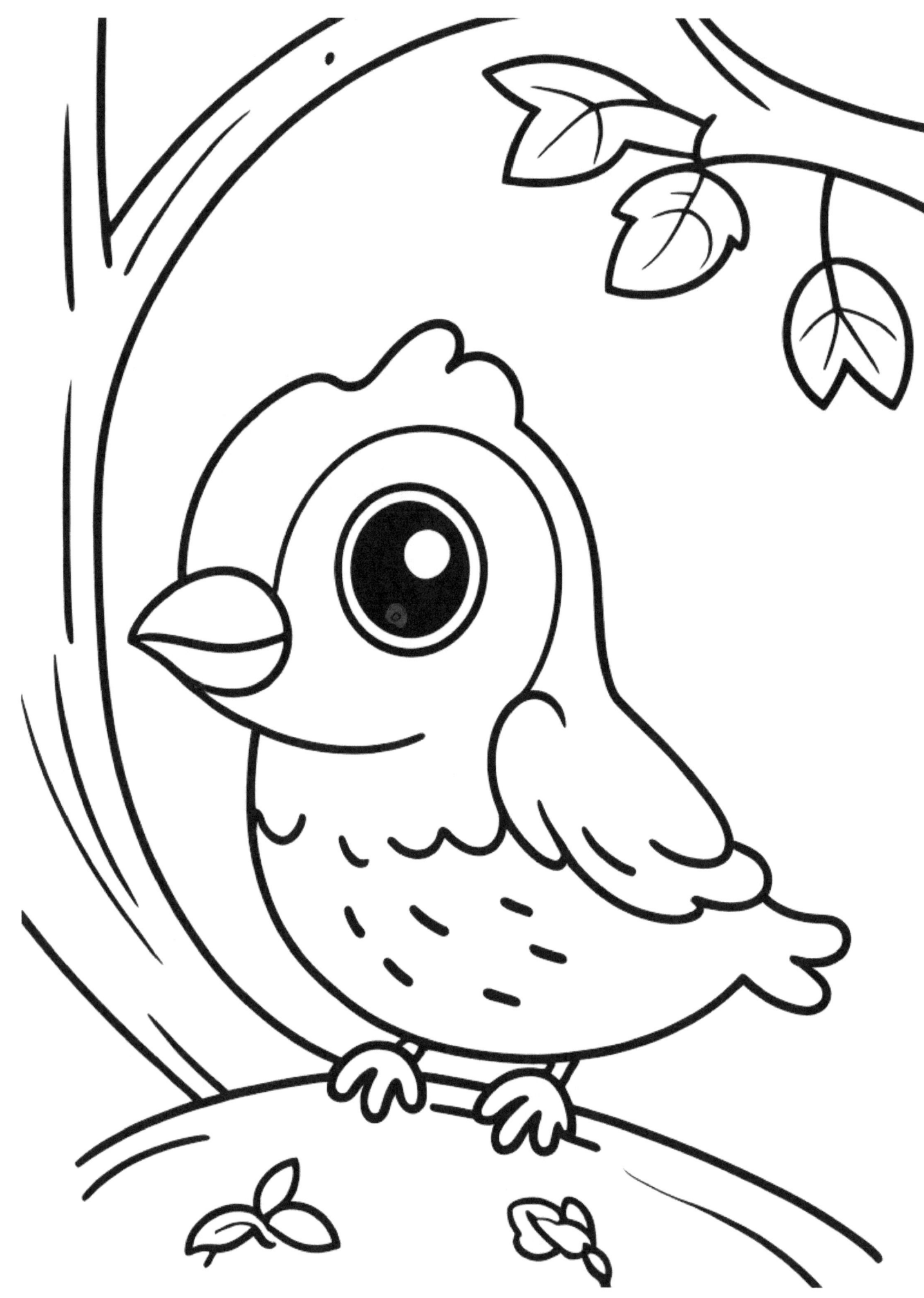

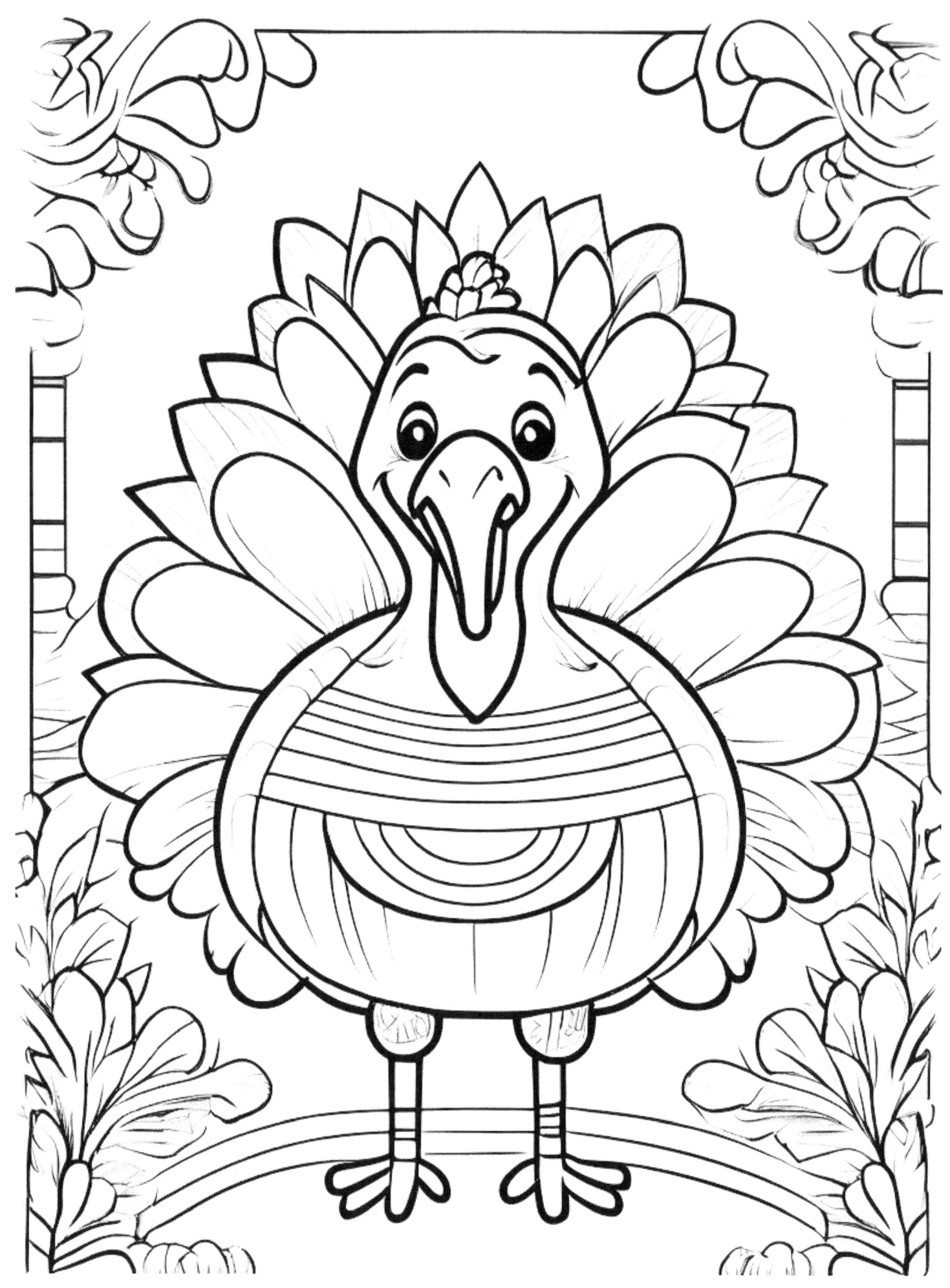

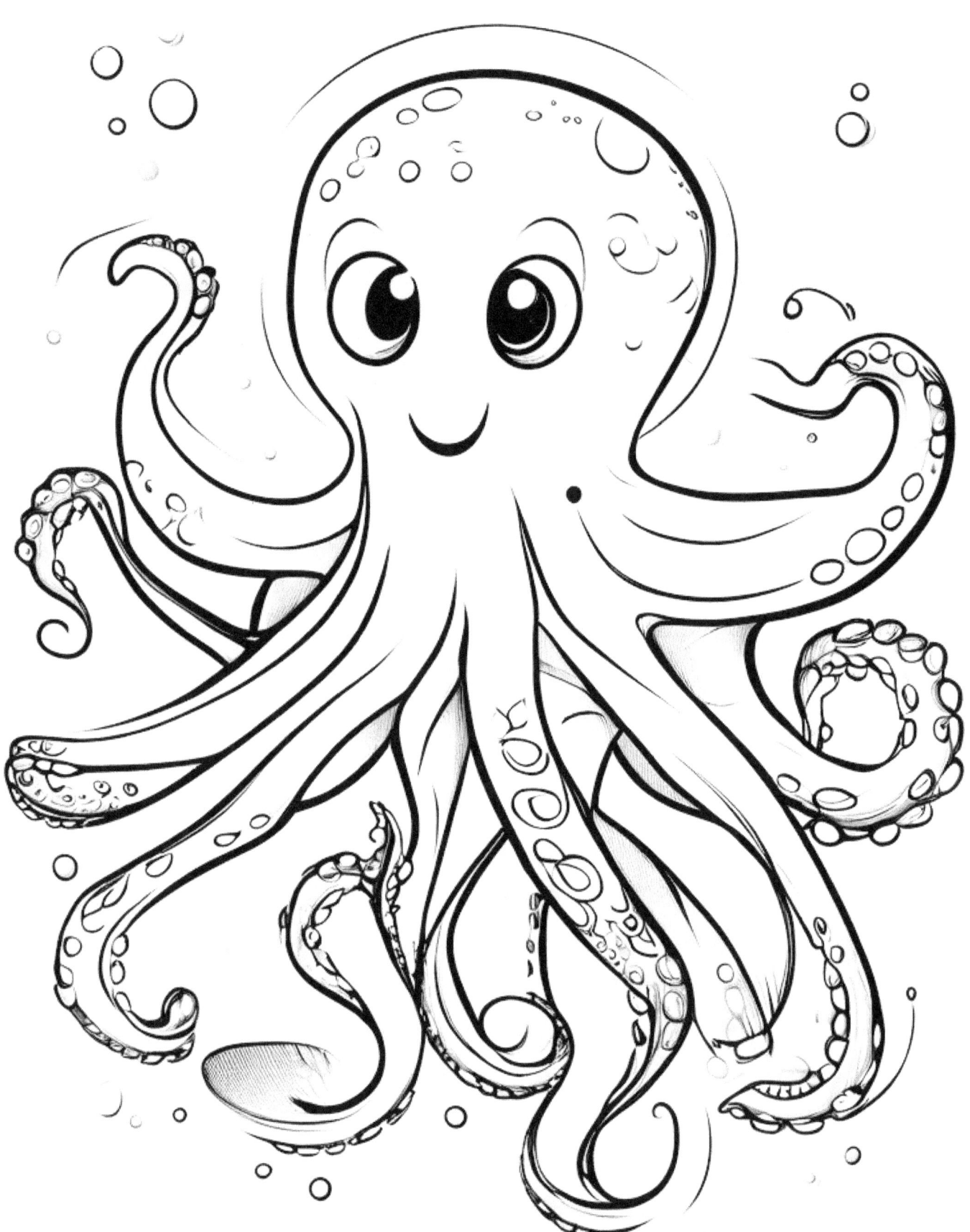

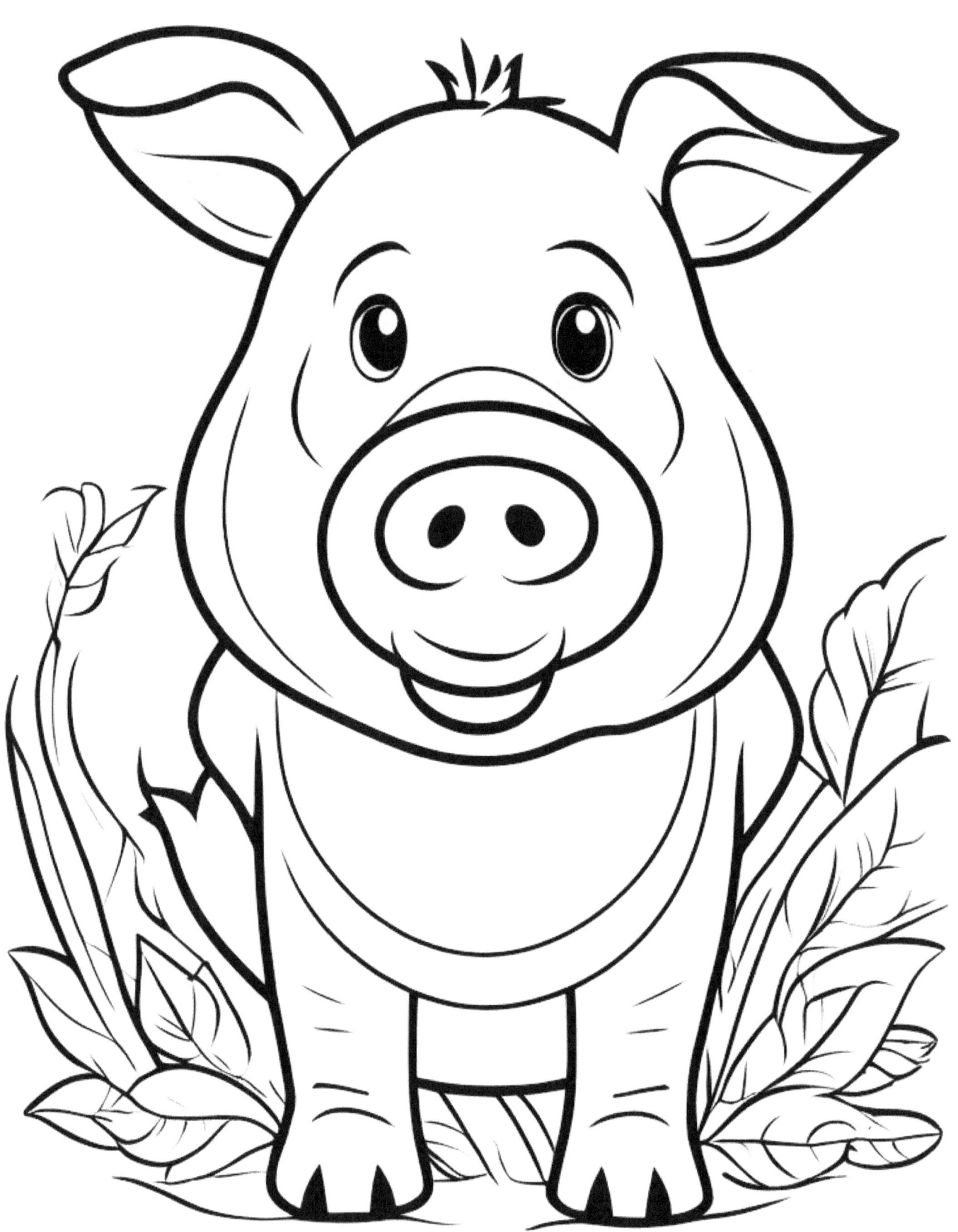

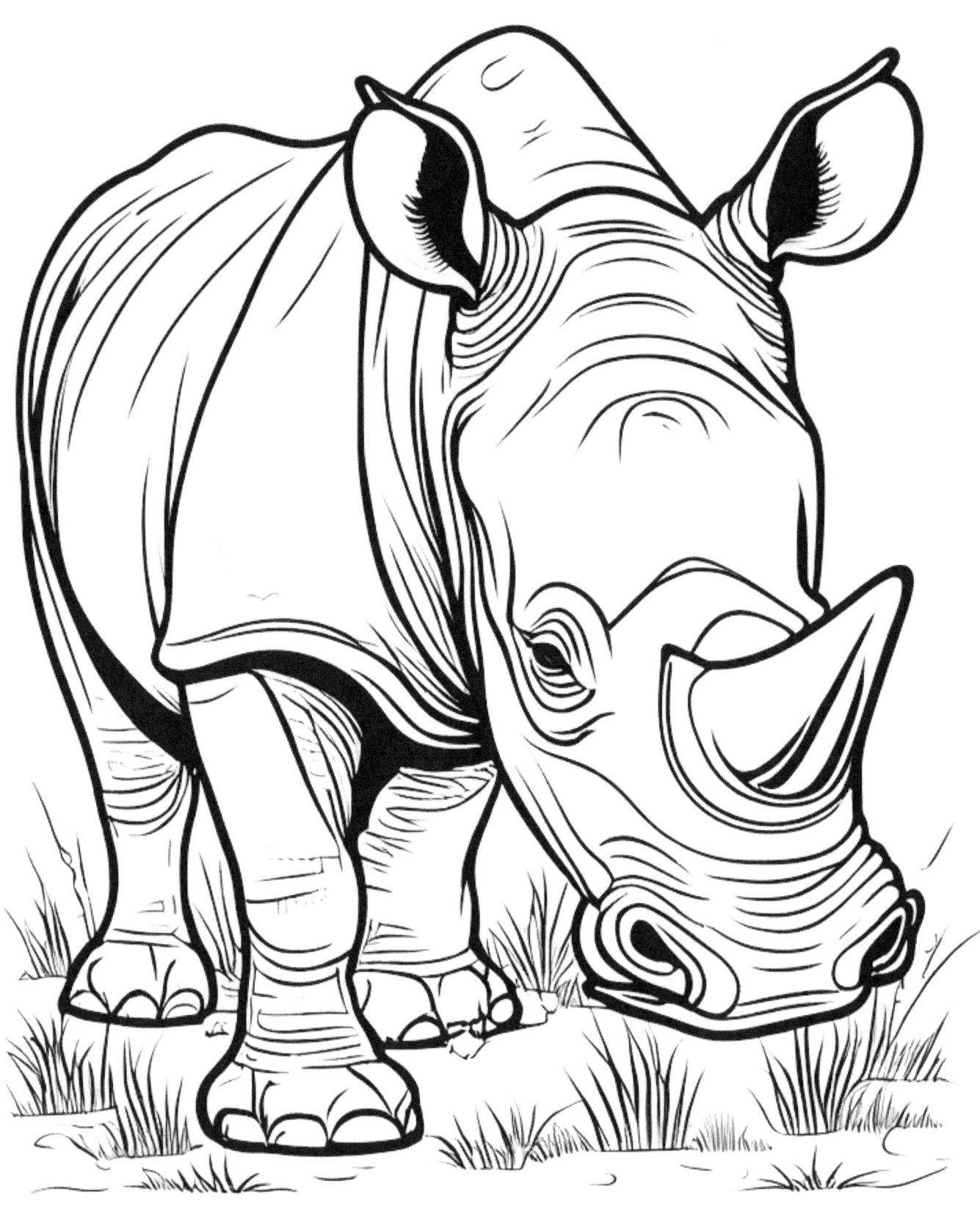

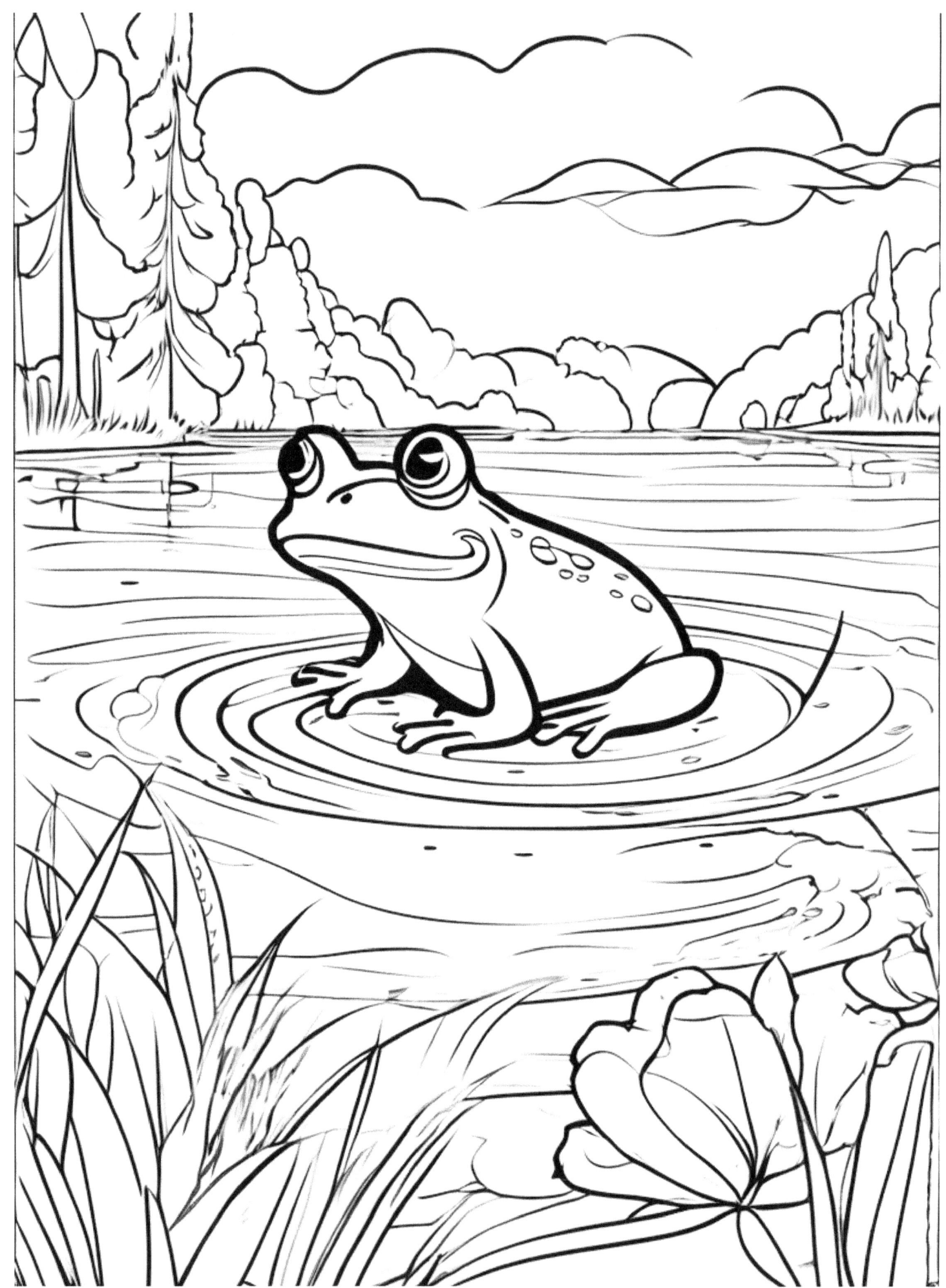

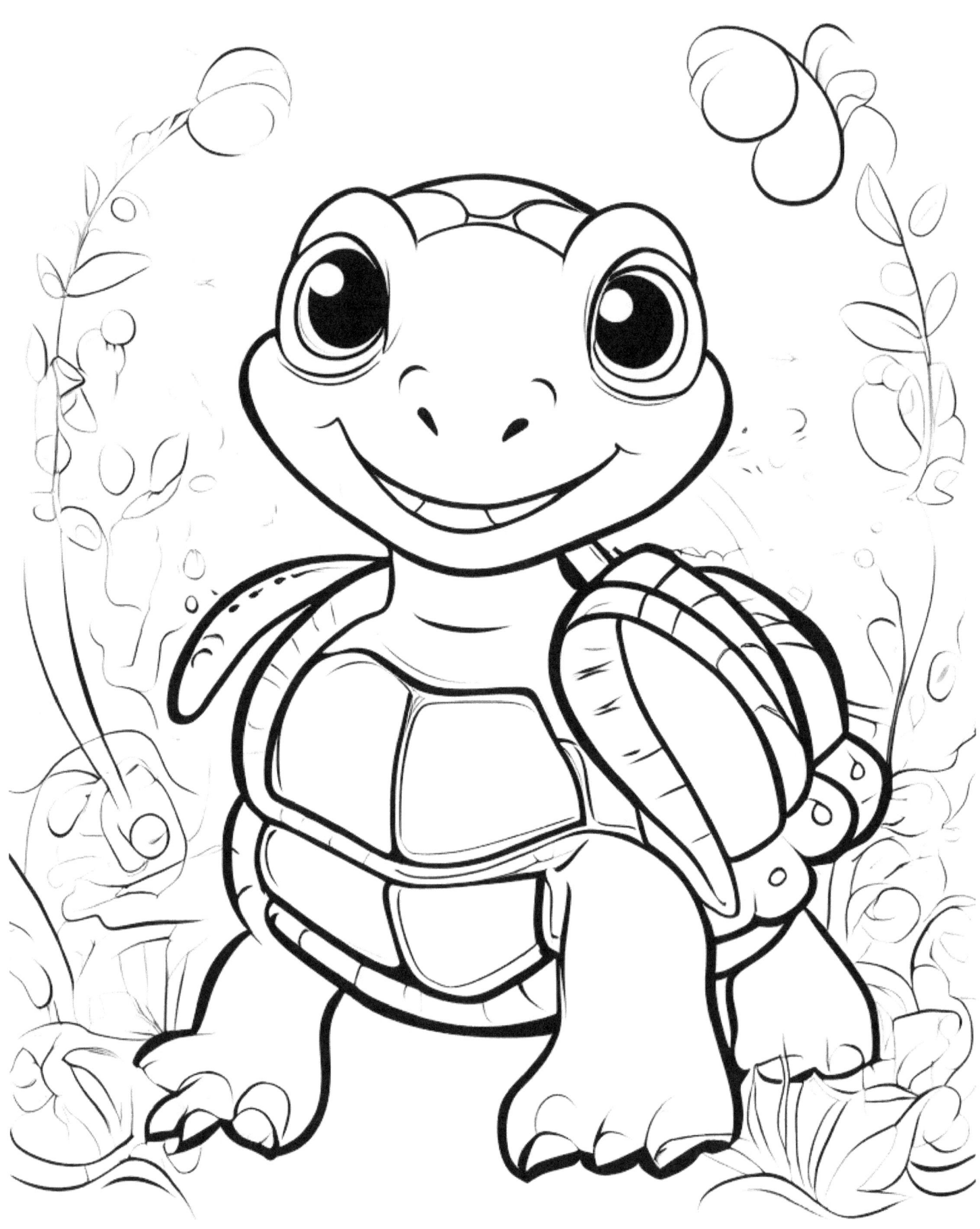

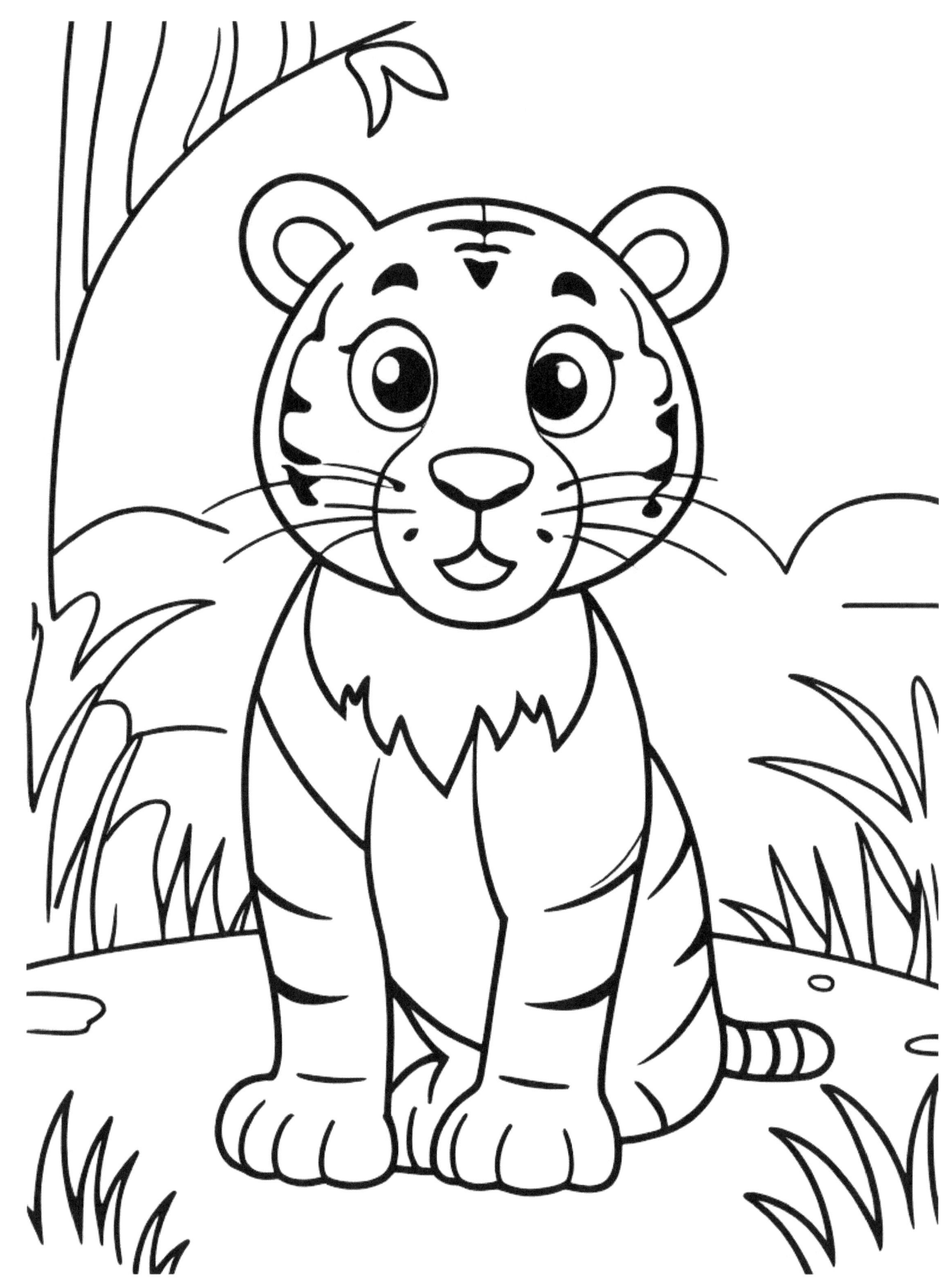

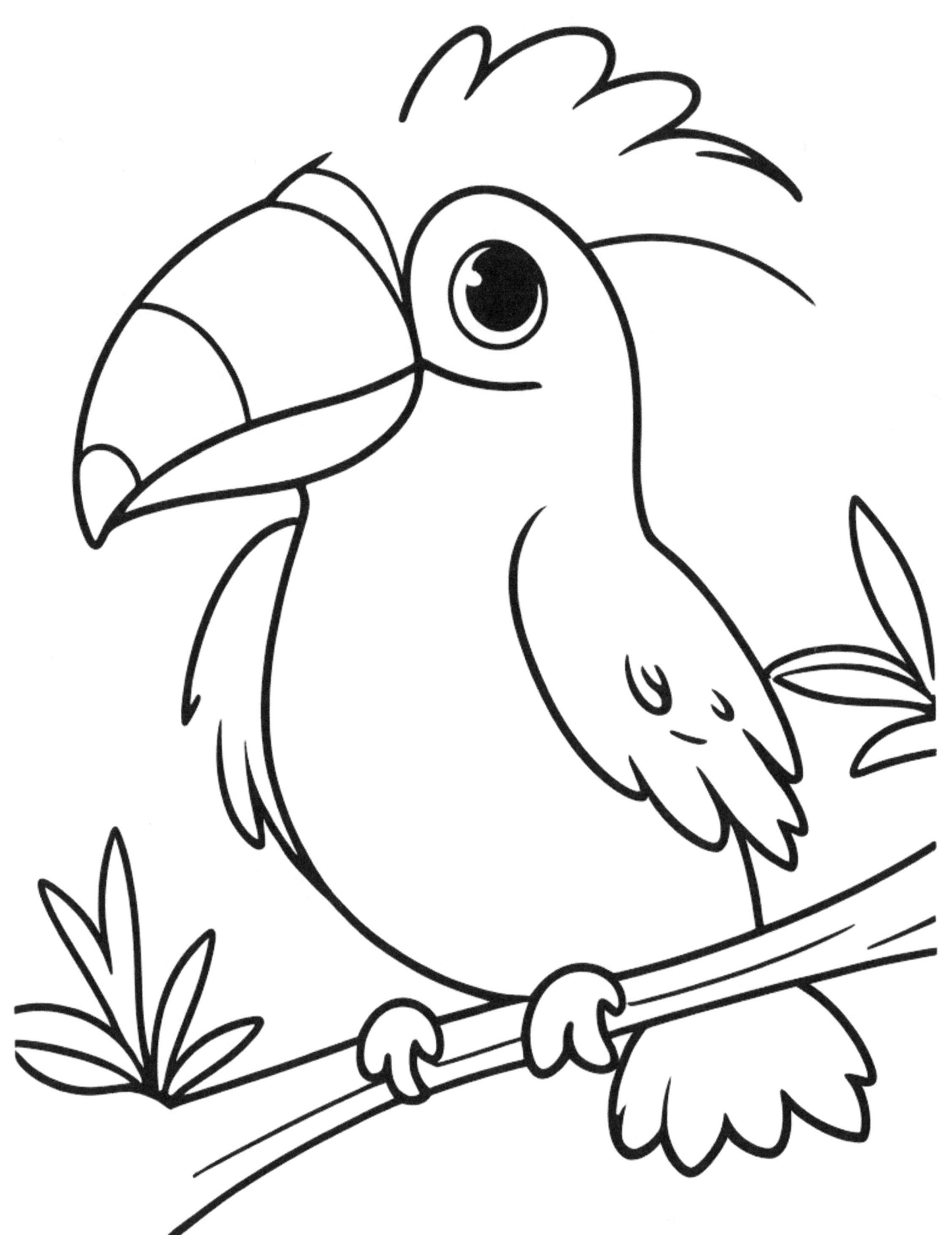

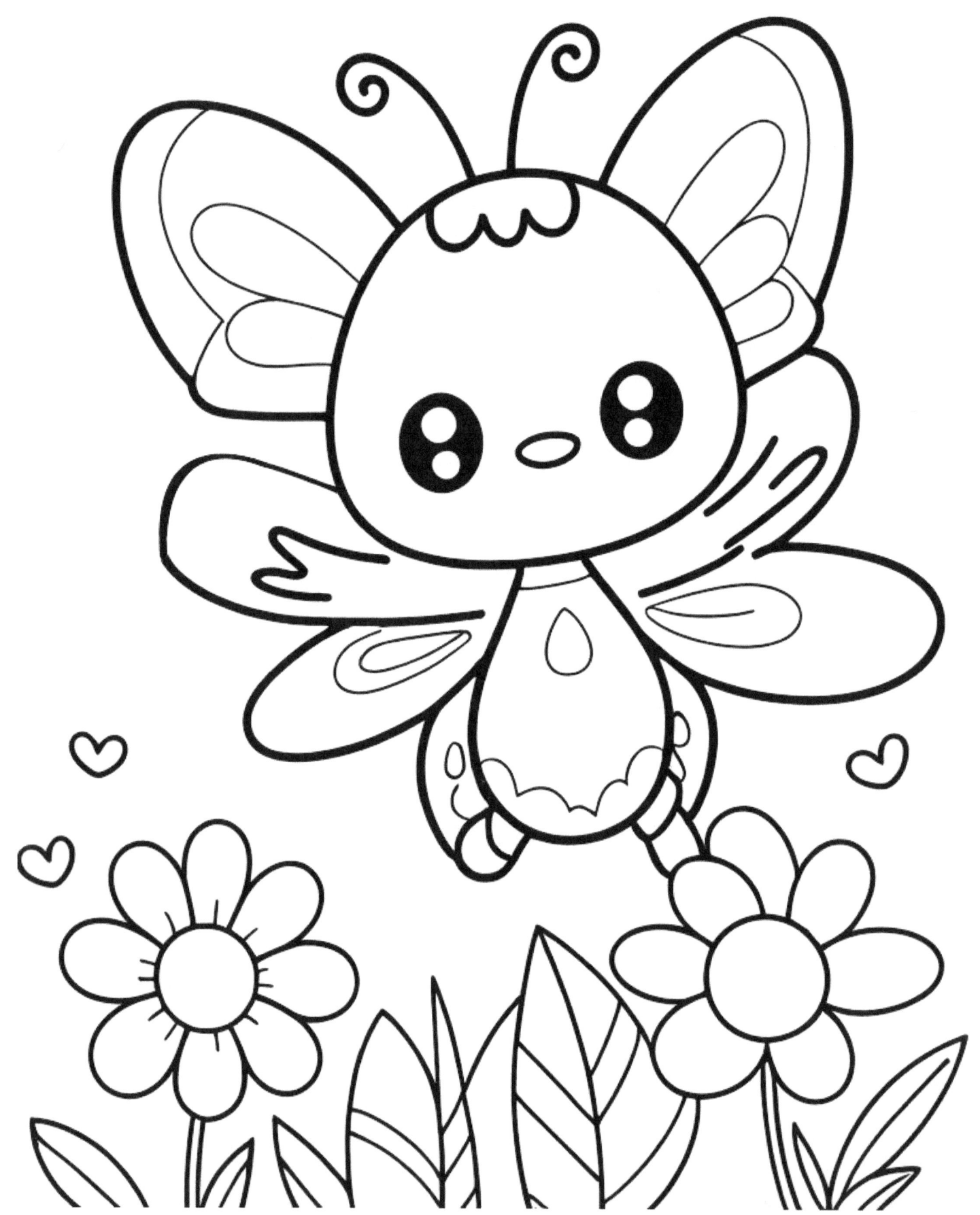

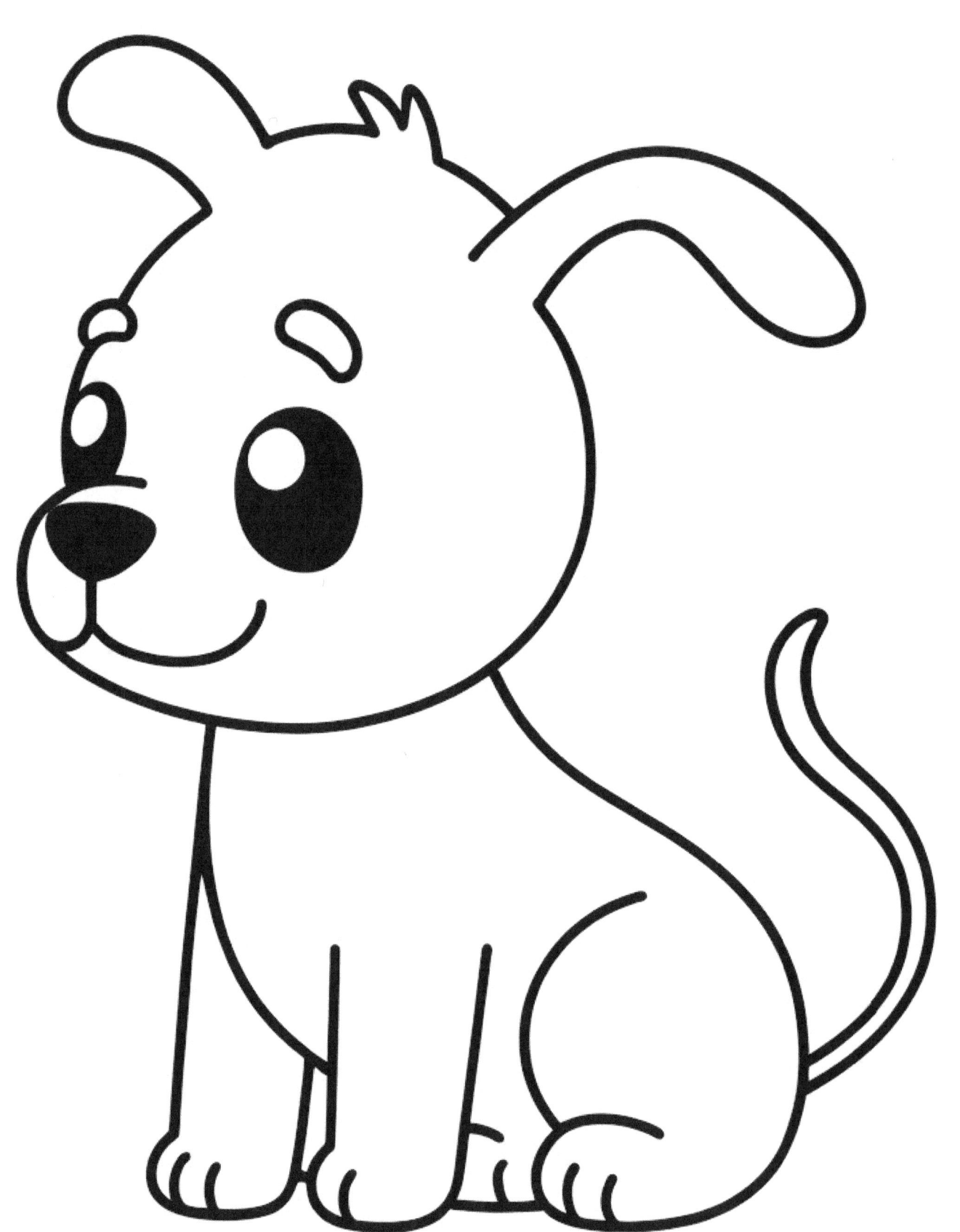

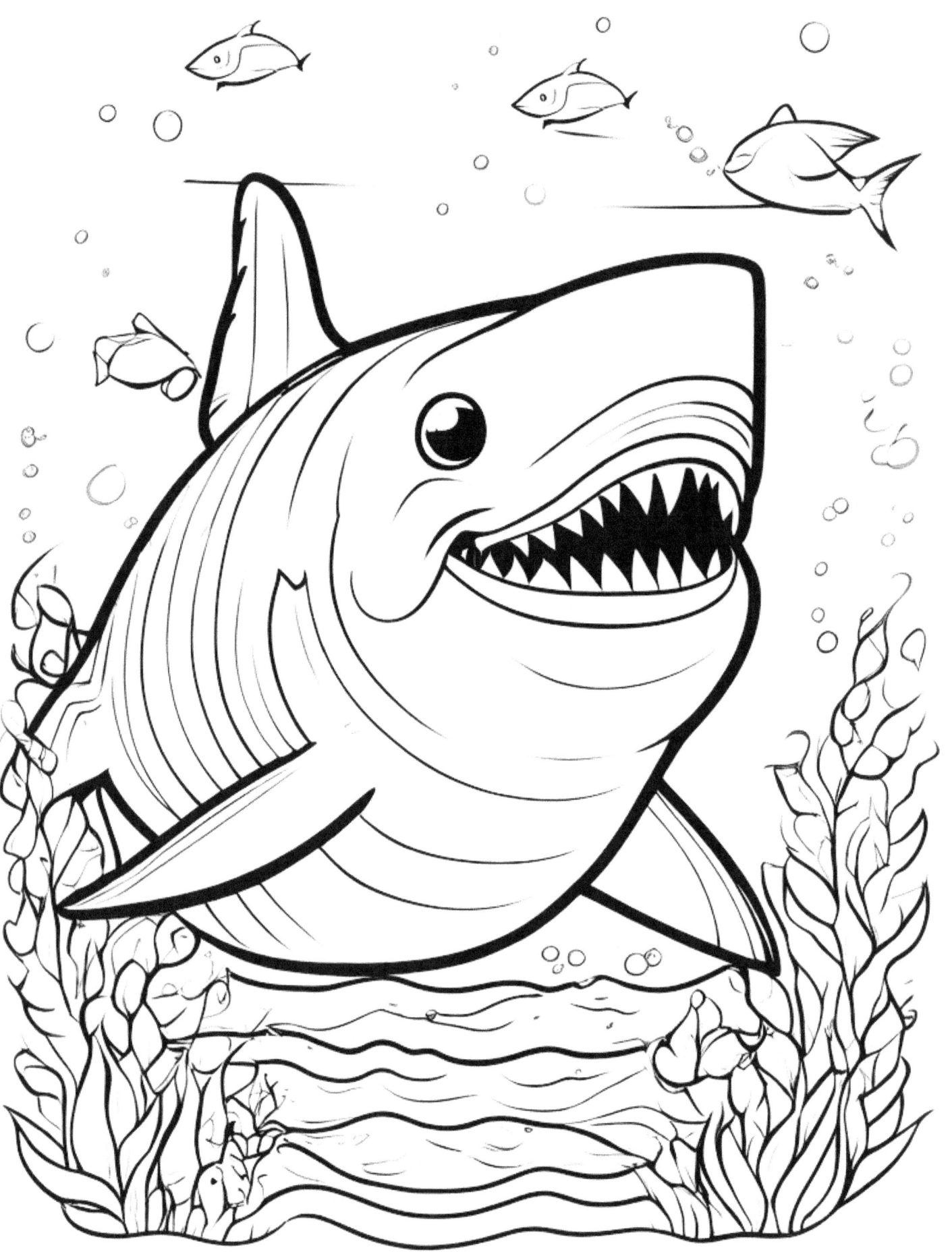

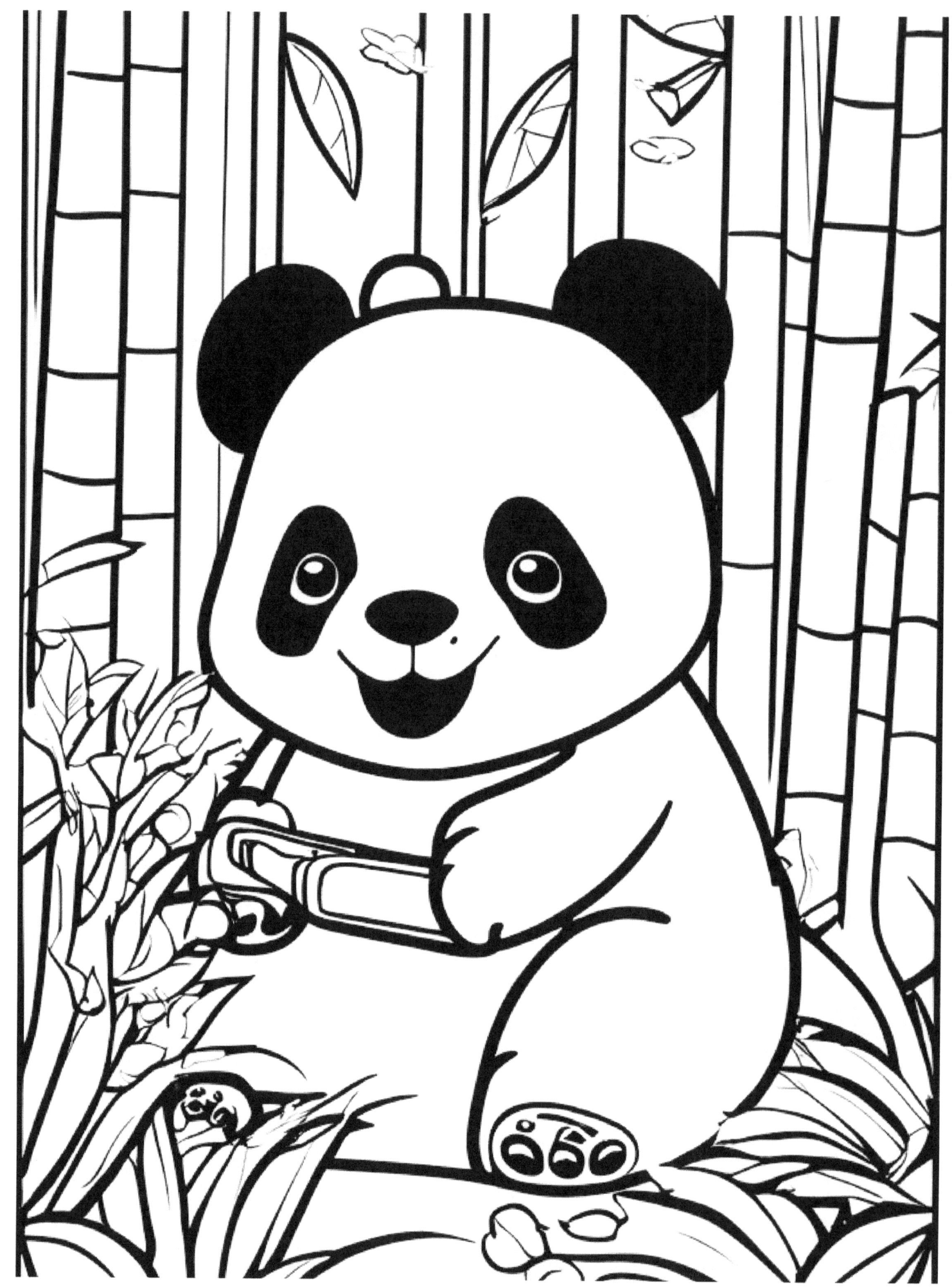

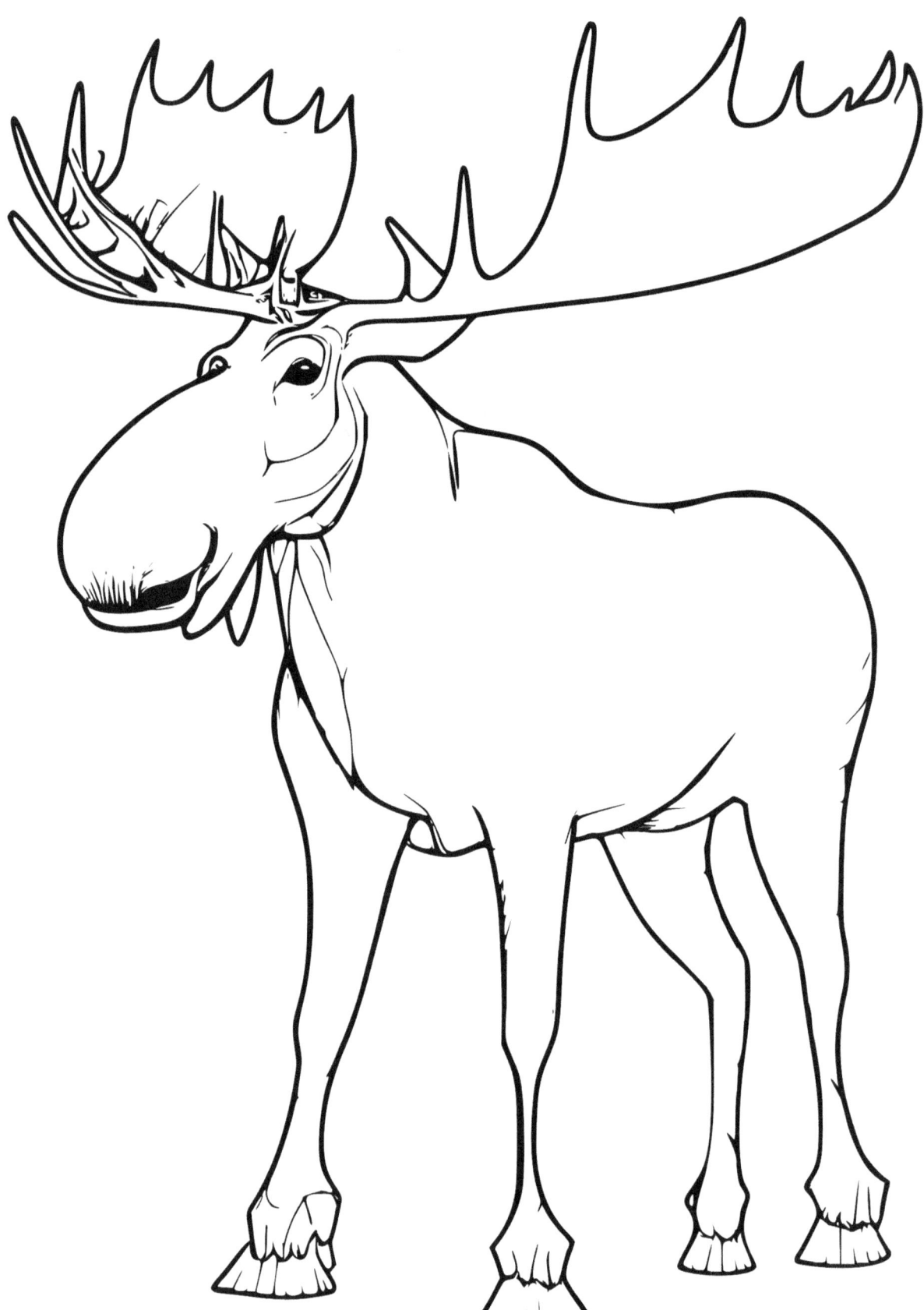